Contents

Foreword
David Attenborough

The first time I saw a swimmer hit a shark on the nose with a camera was in 1956. A film editor in a cutting room next to the one in which I was working burst in excitedly and asked me to come and look at something special. I went next door and there on the flickering screen of his editing machine was the image of a huge shark. He pressed a button. The shark came to life and swam directly towards camera. I could see, only too clearly, rows of white triangular teeth lining its jaws. It came closer and closer until its head filled the screen – the camera lost focus and jolted – there was a brief glimpse of grey flank – and the shark disappeared into blackness.

The film had been shot in the Red Sea, by a young Viennese biologist named Hans Hass. He had been one of the first to take up the newly popular sport of underwater swimming that had recently been made possible by a device called the demand valve. This had been invented during the Second World War by a French naval officer, Jacques Cousteau, and it enabled a swimmer to breathe from compressed air carried in a cylinder strapped to his or her back. With that, a facemask and flippers on the feet, a whole new world had suddenly come within reach of anyone who was reasonably fit.

THE LONG WAIT (below)
Underwater cameraman Daniel Beecham is searching for Indo-Pacific bottlenose dolphins near Mdumbi, off the notoriously dangerous 'Wild Coast' of South Africa.

READY FOR HIS CLOSE UP (above)
Cameraman Gavin Thurston sets
up the next shot with Sir David
Attenborough on a boat off the
Atlantic coast of Florida.

Hans Hass's particular contribution had been to build his own watertight housing for a movie camera so that he could take it with him on his dives and record this new world for everyone to see. It was a huge and unwieldy metal box with a lid with a waterproof seal and a glass plate at the front, close to the lens of the camera within. On the outside there was a stop and start button and a wire rectangle to serve as a crude viewfinder. It took one-hundred-foot rolls of film, so he was only able to shoot a total of two minutes and forty seconds of film before he had to return to the surface, take off the lid, and reload the camera. That could easily take an hour – and much more than that if he had been working at any depth, for then he would be compelled to spend time decompressing on his rise back to the surface. But in spite of these problems, Hass was now shooting a new series of films. It was the first ever underwater series commissioned by the BBC. And when it eventually reached the television screen, it was a sensation – thrilling, revelatory, and often stunningly beautiful.

Much has changed in the sixty years since then. Underwater cameras have become smaller and smaller. Now they shoot not film but video, so they can record hours of material before they need reloading. They are so

sensitive that they can record pictures in depths far beyond the reach of the sun's rays, where the only light is that produced by fish and other deep sea creatures as they find their way around in the pitch blackness. In short, there is virtually no part of the seas that we cannot explore. So at the end of the millennium, teams from the BBC's Natural History unit began work on a series called *Blue Planet*.

Its success was overwhelming both in terms of awards and response from viewers. But no single series could hope to comprehensively cover the undersea world. Now that we could take cameras into almost any part of the seas, how could we tackle stories in even greater detail and more revelatory ways? What were the new stories? Fishermen in the Galápagos Islands noticed that sea lions worked as a team and spread out across hundreds of metres of sea to drive tuna into enclosed bays. We could reveal that by using remotely controlled drones in the skies above. New discoveries have revealed complex communities of strange creatures living within the branches of a coral colony. So the team took lenses that had been developed to film insects in extreme close-up and adapted them to do a similar job underwater. How could we accompany killer whales on their high-speed chases? Use suction cups to attach tiny cameras to the whales' flanks. Low-light cameras that had enabled us to watch lions hunting at night on the plains of Africa were now taken underwater to watch shoals of rays assemble off the coast of Mexico and see how with each beat of their triangular side-fins they produce trails of sparkling plankton glowing in their wake in an underwater ballet of astonishing beauty.

Underwater films have changed a great deal since that first shark bumped its nose on a camera. Now, stand by for *Blue Planet II*, and marvels beyond your imagining.

OUT ON THE DEEP BLUE (right) Sir David Attenborough is aboard the M/V Umbra, a fast support vessel, off the east coast of Florida.

chapter one
One Ocean

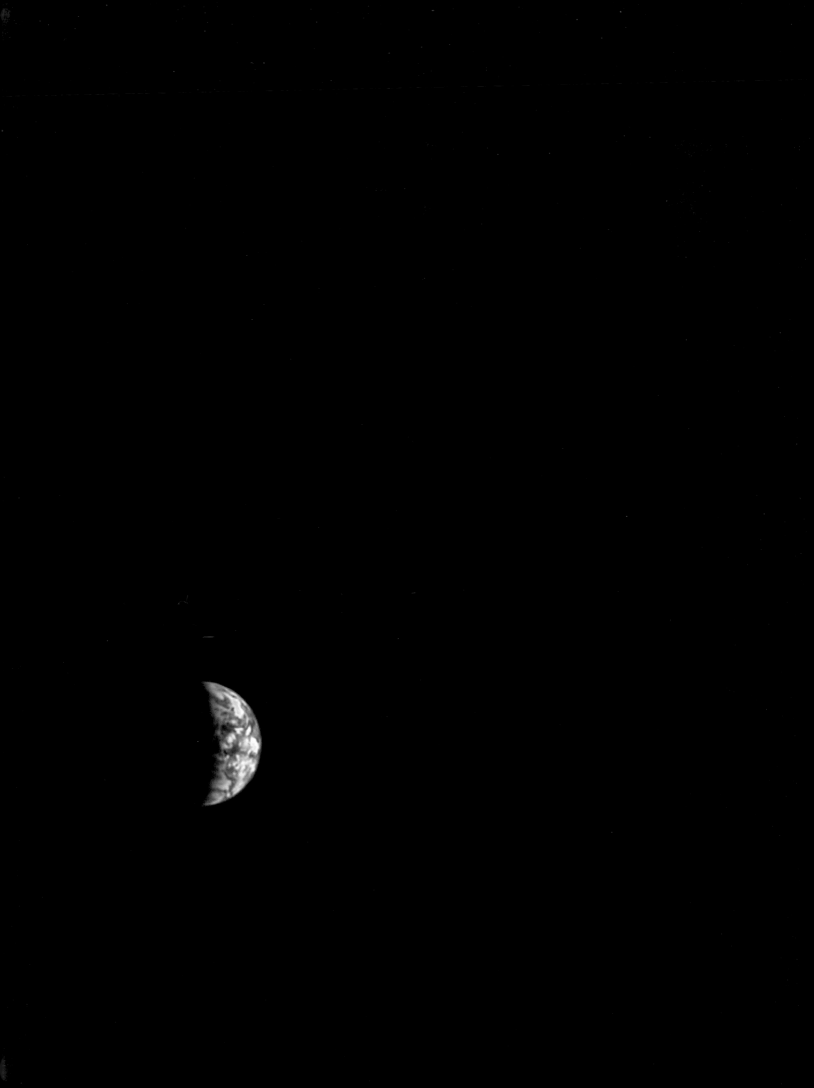

BLUE MARBLE (left) A view of the Earth and Moon from a NASA satellite orbiting the planet Mars, about 225 million kilometres away.

WAKE RIDERS (previous page) Wild bottlenose dolphins ride the wake of a boat near Key Largo, Florida.

S een from NASA's Mars Reconnaissance Orbiter, our blue planet resembles a dappled marble floating in space. Its blueness is what makes the Earth unique – the presence of water, and lots of it. Other planets and their moons may have water hidden from view, but our planet has vast quantities of liquid water on its surface. Where it came from, nobody is sure. Water could have been released from the rocks that formed the Earth, its origin in the disc of dust from which the planets of the solar system were made approximately 4.5 billion years ago, or asteroids and comets could have delivered it. Whichever way it came, most of it is here to stay, because the Earth is in the 'Goldilocks Zone': it is neither too hot nor too cold, but just the right distance from the sun for water not to freeze or boil off into space.

Today, that water covers about 71 per cent of our planet's surface, and 96.54 per cent of all the Earth's free water is in the ocean, yet 95 per cent of that is unexplored. The reason is not hard to see: the oceans are among the most inaccessible and expensive places to study. Nevertheless, these logistical and financial stumbling blocks have not stopped the pace of human endeavour. Ingenuity, painstaking research and recent advances in marine technology and engineering are enabling scientists to explore the seas as never before; yet, ironically, it was our ventures into space, rather than underwater, that alerted us to the key role the oceans play in maintaining the health of our planet.

Although the oceans have been studied since ancient times, it was not until we put satellites into Earth orbit and looked back at our planet that we began to appreciate their role in its wellbeing. The oceans are the Earth's life-support system. They help regulate the amount of oxygen and carbon dioxide in the air we breathe, influence our weather and the climate, and so deliver the water we drink, provide a substantial amount of the food we eat, and they could be the reason we are here at all: the origins of life could well have been in the sea.

South African Super-Groups

People have always been drawn to the sea and humbled by its power, yet have been largely ignorant of what lies beneath its surface, but in recent times all that has been changing. One reason has been an international initiative called the Census of Marine Life, an exciting period of marine research that set out to document how many different kinds of animals live in the oceans, where they live, how many there are, and what threatens them. And what a study it has turned out to be: more than 6,000 possible new species of marine life discovered, extraordinary migrations and mind-blowing behaviours revealed, and the follow-up work has not stopped. New discoveries keep coming every day, like the sudden appearance of unusually large numbers of humpback whales feeding off the southwest coast of South Africa.

The first of these super-groups was spotted in 2011, and they have reappeared in subsequent years. Filmed for the 'Green Seas' episode, each gathering can have up to 200 whales occupying a small patch of sea, and another surprise is that the whales are here during the summer months. Southern hemisphere whales generally head for the Antarctic to feed on the dense swarms of Antarctic krill that occur there in summer, but here they feed on a smaller type of krill, together with amphipods and mantis shrimps, in the nutrient-rich waters of the southern Benguela Current system.

Why the whales gather here and in such numbers can only be speculation for now, but the scientists observing them suggest that they are witnessing events that were more common before the twentieth-century whaling industry reduced the world population to fewer than 5,000 individuals. Since 1966, when commercial whaling for humpbacks ceased, their populations have been slowly rebuilding.

One reason for these aggregations might be that their numbers have reached a critical threshold and they are starting to revert to pre-whaling behaviour. Other explanations are that they might be shifting their behaviour in response to the abundance of prey in this rich ecosystem, or they have been forced to find new feeding opportunities because the population increase has created stiff competition for food down south. Now scientists are planning to track the whales to fathom out just why these humpbacks seemed to have changed their annual migration.

HUMPBACK GATHERING (right) Large numbers of humpback whales feed together off the South African coast.

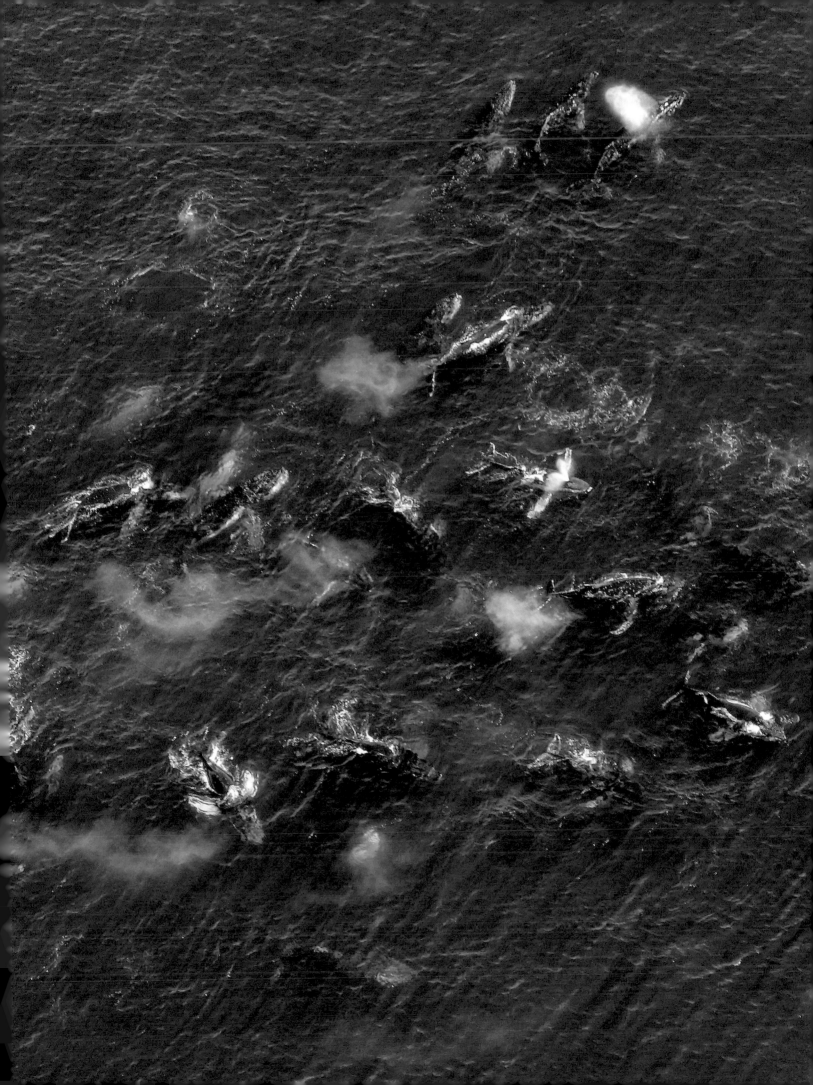

Hand in Hand

South Africa's whale mystery is one of many discoveries made since the *Blue Planet* television series was broadcast nearly two decades ago. Now *Blue Planet II* explores the world's ocean, with production teams having searched for and filmed the deadliest, cleverest and most charismatic marine creatures on Earth.

They have undertaken 125 expeditions and spent 1,500 days at sea, including more than 1,000 hours in the deep. They have filmed in every ocean, at many depths, off every continent, visiting coral reefs, coasts, undersea forests and meadows, the deep sea, and the vast open ocean. They have even added to the fund of scientific knowledge. New recording techniques, such as miniature on-board cameras attached directly to animals, observe behaviour from their perspective, and drones give a grandstand view of events unfolding below. The use of 're-breathers', a form of breathing apparatus that makes fewer bubbles has enabled the film crews to remain underwater for up to five hours at a time and so record complex animal behaviour up close, without disturbing it.

These techniques have enabled teams to contribute directly to ongoing research, and their work features in newly published scientific papers. It has meant that many of the stories in *Blue Planet II* are entirely new to science and were filmed for television for the very first time. At Lizard Island on Australia's Great Barrier Reef, for example, an intriguing piece of behaviour has been taking place right under the noses of scientists studying marine life around the island, and, it has gone unnoticed until quite recently. It reveals a surprising relationship between an animal with a backbone and one without.

PREPARE TO DIVE (below) One of the two manned submersibles used by *Blue Planet II* film crews is ready to be launched from the stern of its mother ship, *Alucia*.

UNUSUAL CLAPPERBOARD (right) One of the coral reef stars of *Blue Planet II* is reassured it's on the right show. Marine biologist Dr Alex Vail is at Lizard Island on the Great Barrier Reef.

DEEP DIVER (far right) A manned submersible, with producer aboard, probes the darkness of the deep sea.

CLOWNFISH CLOSE-UP (below right) Underwater cameraman Roger Munns uses an underwater straight scope system for close-up shots of the clownfish family at Mabul Island, southeast Sabah, Malaysia.

An Unlikely Alliance

The coral trout is a grumpy-looking member of the grouper family, and it appears to confront a reef octopus out of its lair. Soft-bodied octopuses are vulnerable out in the open, but the coral trout is mainly a fish-eater, so the octopus seems unperturbed. The grouper appears interested in a small fish or crustacean hidden under a branching coral, but it is too big to get at it. It swims slowly back and forth, and then manoeuvres so that its head points down at the crevice in which the target is hiding. It shakes its head back and forth, pointing deliberately at the potential meal. The octopus responds, its soft and highly flexible arms enabling it to probe the crack that the large fish is unable to enter, and flushes out the prey, which one of them grabs.

'The first time that I saw a coral trout hunting with an octopus, I was absolutely gobsmacked,' recollects Alex Vail at the Lizard Island Research Station. He has been studying the collaboration between groupers and other species, which includes octopuses, moray eels and large wrasse. He found that sometimes the octopus is successful and at other times the grouper grabs the prize, but both do better by hunting together than by working alone.

WORKING TOGETHER (below) At Lizard Island, the coral trout points to prey hiding in a tight crevice, and the reef octopus drifts in to flush it out.

FISH FRIENDS (above) A coral grouper teams up with a moray eel. The eel's long and slender body enables it to probe into crevices in the reef that are inaccessible to the grouper.

It is surprising behaviour. Both animals must have learned it. Octopuses are known for their intelligence, but most fish generally are not. This fish, however, has learned to point. It uses a sign language, dubbed the 'headstand signal', to reach across the vertebrate-invertebrate divide and encourage another species to help it hunt. Until now, this kind of gesturing behaviour has been associated mainly with apes and birds in the crow family, such as ravens, but several species of groupers are now known to 'point'.

In the Red Sea, for example, roving coral groupers team up with giant moray eels, but not all eels play along, so the gesturing grouper must also learn which individuals are worth asking for help and then return to them time and again.

Fish have small brains for their body size compared, say, to primates, so the big question for scientists is how fish can carry out complicated tasks like these with such limited brainpower. However, although the animals cooperate, it is thought that individual interests ultimately drive the behaviour, a way to gain an advantage on the highly competitive tropical coral reef. Nevertheless, we may have to redefine the way we look at some forms of marine life. 'I think the general idea has been that fish don't think much at all,' says Alex, 'but fish really are thinking.'

While these two characters demonstrate a new understanding of the interdependence of marine creatures within a defined habitat like a tropical coral reef, another 'first-time-for-television' story explores the connection between two very different worlds, one above the waves, the other below. It occurs in October on a small island in the Indian Ocean. Like the grouper and octopus, it has probably been going on unnoticed for many years. Only now can its story be told.

Fish Missiles

On a tiny island in the Seychelles, about 400,000 pairs of sooty terns arrive to nest in August and September each year. They choose to come here because it is remote and free from terrestrial predators, and the lagoons and shallow waters around the coral island are teeming with the staple diet of terns. Terns are shallow divers that catch small fish close to the surface, and one way they can do this is to shadow the larger predatory fish, such as giant trevally. The big fish drive schools of smaller fish towards the surface and, in their desperate attempts to escape the jaws of the trevally, they fall prey to swooping terns.

In October, when parents are weary from feeding their chicks and the burgeoning tick population is unbearable, the young terns abandon their nests and must find food for themselves. They take to the air on unsteady wings, and the winds can be very blustery, so sometimes the birds fail to keep aloft. They ditch in the sea. Bad mistake. Slam! Out of nowhere a huge fish grabs a fledgling and pulls it below. It is a giant trevally, and it has turned the tables. Instead of bird watching fish, fish watches bird.

At up to 1.7 metres long, giant trevallies are real titans. The biggest of the jack family, they have large, extendable jaws, and their behaviour in the Seychelles is reminiscent of the tiger sharks that take Laysan albatross fledglings at French Frigate Shoals, except that the trevally have one up on the tigers: they catch birds in mid-air. Filming all this, however, was a leap of faith for *Blue Planet II* producer Miles Barton.

'This was the first time in twenty-five years of filmmaking that I set out to film an event of which so little was known. We were told that a friend of a friend of a friend had seen the fish leaping from the water, and we tracked down the original source – a group of big game fishermen who go for these feisty predators on this remote atoll; so, it was a big risk committing a film crew to fly halfway across the world on mere hearsay. Nevertheless, when we arrived we were relieved to find fish leaping all over the place, but it was happening so quickly and randomly it was impossible for cameraman Ted Giffords to have the camera pointing at the right place.

'Fortunately, local fishing guide Peter King has an intimate knowledge of the fish's behaviour, and he led us to his daily lunch spot, a beach overlooking a channel where the fish gather at high tide. Ted could then see their outlines underwater, Peter could predict where a fish would strike, and what stunning behaviour we recorded.'

Giant trevally have exceptional eyesight and panoramic vision, and they congregate at key places in the clear waters on the lagoon side of

READY TO LAUNCH (below) A giant trevally watches out for young terns overhead. It's a smart fish, and is also known to shadow seals and sharks to catch their escaping prey.

TAKE-OFF (opposite) A giant trevally launches into the air, but, thanks to the tern's exquisite aerobatics, the fish is unsuccessful in bringing down the bird.

the atoll, where they can see the silhouettes of a steady stream of birds overhead. As a tern flies low or hovers over the water, the trevally erupts from the surface. It knocks the tern out of the sky or grabs the bird in its mouth, drags it below and swallows it.

'The fish creates a bow wave above it, tracking the bird from below,' Miles could see. 'Sometimes it decides the fish is too high and goes no further. However, if the bird stoops close enough to the water, the giant trevally launches itself like a missile and expands its mouth to the size of a football to enclose the bird and bring it down. To see a metre-long fish leave the water and take down a fully grown tern is a dramatic sight, but some of the more exciting views were when the fish committed itself, but the bird, through incredible aerobatics, escaped at the last moment.'

'The hunting tactic seemed to depend on the size of fish,' researcher Sophie Morgan noticed. 'The smaller fish made the most dramatic leaps, and despite their exuberance they missed the birds a surprising number of times. I guess it takes too much energy for the bigger fish to propel their

ISLAND PARADISE (above) The sooty tern colony and lagoon in the Seychelles.

CAPTURE THE MOMENT (above)
Cameraman Ted Giffords waits in the lagoon for giant trevally to leap out and grab the young sooty terns.

huge bodies out of the water and perhaps they have learned that they have a better hit rate by targeting terns on or close to the water.'

While filming the trevallies erupting from the surface like this gave Miles and his team the top half of their story, they also wanted to see how the fish behave underwater, and, for underwater cameraman Dan Beecham, this turned out to be a tad uncomfortable.

'Giant trevallies normally pose little threat to people, but, even so, getting into the water with them was rather daunting. They are really large fish and apex predators with extremely powerful jaws.'

And the crew saw what damage those jaws could do.

'These giant fish had become used to fishermen throwing scraps into the water and would attack anything that made a splash,' recalls Miles, 'so everybody moved slowly and gingerly, and the fish would simply circle, giving us wonderful shots of their bulldog-like faces. When a guide accidentally dropped a soft drinks can, though, the fish were on it in an instant. The puncture marks were a reminder not to put a foot wrong!'

Out of the Blue

Off the coast of New Zealand, false killer whales have thrown up another big surprise for watching scientists. False killers are actually large dolphins, and they have a bad reputation because, like their namesakes, they sometimes harass other cetaceans. Pods have been known to attack smaller dolphin species and there is one report of them killing a humpback whale calf. Even giant sperm whales are not immune. The false killers worry them until they regurgitate their hard-earned deep-sea squid, so the prospect of an encounter between false killers and bottlenose dolphins with calves is potentially explosive.

The dolphins are travelling near North Island, the false killers not far behind. The larger cetaceans had split into two groups and spent some time apart in the open ocean, but now they have rejoined into a formidable force, about 150 strong.

The bottlenose dolphins chatter to each other, mothers reassuring their calves with sequences of clicks, whistles and whines, while the calves answer back, but the false killers have eavesdropped on their intimate conversations from as far away as 30 kilometres and have locked on. The pursuers increase their speed, powering along at a steady 10 knots. The gap closes and suddenly they are on them... then something quite extraordinary happens.

The false killers and the bottlenose dolphins intermingle, touching and greeting each other like old friends. Incredibly, the bottlenose dolphins appear to adjust their calls when they are with the false killers off New Zealand, raising the tantalising possibility that they may be able to communicate with each other across the species boundary.

Individual animals seem able to recognise each other, and may even form long-lasting relationships, and, as they mill about, they begin

AERIAL VIEW (below) Helicopters were used to follow the fast-moving pods off the north coast of New Zealand.

BEST OF PALS (opposite) Bottlenose dolphins and false killer whales meet in the ocean and hunt together. The dolphins are 2–4 metres long, while the false killers are up to 6 metres long. Both live in temperate and tropical waters throughout the world.

'One thing that stands out for me is how noisy they are. You feel the reverberation through your body. And they're not concerned about personal space.'

STEVE HATHAWAY, Underwater Cameraman

to organise themselves, ready to go hunting. The two species form into smaller mixed sub-groups, like best friends getting together, and these groups can spread across several kilometres of ocean.

Together they go in search of shoals of large fish. This is their strategy for success. By forming this unusual alliance and casting their net wider, they become far more effective at finding and catching prey that is distributed unevenly in the ocean, and competition is not a problem because there is plenty for all. An added bonus is the many more eyes and ears alert to the presence of their mutual enemies – killer whales and great white sharks.

And, when the hunting is over, it's time to rest. The false killer whales form a tightknit resting group, so the bottlenose dolphins must mill about on the periphery.

'One thing that stands out for me is how noisy they are,' recalls underwater cameraman Steve Hathaway. 'You feel the reverberation through your body. And they're not concerned about personal space. They gather together in a tightly packed pod with barely any space between them.'

False killers are one of the least studied cetaceans. They live in the warmer parts of the open ocean, where they might travel up to 200 kilometres in a day, but sometimes come inshore like the New Zealand groups. They reach a grand old age of 60 or more years, as long as they avoid getting tangled in fishing gear. They are not common, even in their known haunts, and this unusual behaviour with their pals the dolphins has helped to focus the scientific spotlight on them. Is the behaviour of mutual benefit, or is one species exploiting the other?

'False killers are incredibly charismatic,' says researcher Jochen Zaeschmar, who has been closely following these mixed groups, 'and I am glad that they are finally getting the wider recognition they deserve. To me, fully understanding the relationship between the two species is the most intriguing part of our research.'

Surf's Up!

Dolphins like to surf. There's no doubt about it. Up to 100 bottlenose dolphins have been seen to form a line close to the shore on surfing coasts in Western Australia and South Africa, just like human surfers waiting for the next big one. They ride with the wave, pulling out as it breaks on the beach, before heading back for more. Why dolphins surf is a mystery, but even rational, down-to-earth scientists have been forced to admit that it looks as if they're simply having fun.

The waves on which they surf have their origin far out at sea. Most are a product of the wind, although landslides and earthquakes can produce them too. The wind blows, air molecules rub against water molecules and energy is transferred from wind to waves. The stronger the wind, the bigger the waves, and the longer the 'fetch' – the distance over which the wind blows – the more energy a wave can build up. The largest significant wave height ever recorded by a data buoy in the open ocean was 19 metres. This was the average height of a series of large waves that formed between Iceland and the UK. They were logged on 4 February 2013.

AERIAL DOLPHINS (above) Bottlenose dolphins perform an 'aerial'. They launch into the air while surfing large waves.

ANGLING DOLPHINS (overleaf) The dolphins ride across the surface of the wave, rather than straight towards the beach.

When they reach the coast, these large waves can be even more impressive. As the water is pushed towards the shore, the bottom of the wave drags on the seabed, so the upper part moves faster than the lower part, shortening the length and increasing the wave's height. As the depth decreases, the drag on the wave bottom increases and the crest topples forward and eventually curls, creating a crash of foaming water – the breaker.

Most of the largest breaking waves occur on coasts facing the wrath of the ocean. It is the place advanced surfers like to be, such as Nazaré in Portugal, where the Atlantic Ocean surges up a submarine canyon and delivers waves the height of office blocks, up to 30 metres tall. It is one of the wildest and most dangerous surfing locations in the world, and it is not for the faint-hearted. Waves like these crash into cliffs like a fast-moving car hitting a brick wall. On impact, tiny pockets of air trapped in cracks and crevices are compressed to such an extent they trigger mini-explosions. It can sculpt rocks, destroy buildings and kill people, and the bad news is that waves now appear to be getting even bigger and more powerful.

Monster Waves and Black Holes

STORM AT SEA (opposite) During a storm, the fishing vessel *Ocean Harvest* ploughs through exceptionally high waves in the North Sea.

POWERFUL WAVES (below) High winds, blowing over a long fetch, create large, destructive waves that erode the coastline.

Alongside the remarkable discoveries that scientists have been making about the behaviour of marine life are more disturbing revelations about the marine environment in which it lives. Oceanographers and climatologists are warning that many of their new discoveries reflect a rapidly changing world, and they are not all for the good.

A warming planet, widely believed to be caused by raised carbon dioxide levels in the atmosphere from the burning of fossil fuels, means that sea surface temperatures are increasing. The likely consequences are fiercely debated. In some models, tropical storms – hurricanes, typhoons and cyclones – are predicted to increase in intensity. There will be fewer of them, according to research by Florida State University, for example, but each storm is more powerful than it would have been in the past and lasts for longer. Coupled with this, scientists report a general increase in ocean wind speeds and wave heights.

Oceanographers at Swinburne University of Technology, Melbourne, have looked at data from 1985 to 2008 and have found that, off Western Australia, wind speeds have increased by 10 per cent during the past couple of decades and extreme wave heights are 6 metres on average today, compared to just 1 metre in 1985. Similar increases have been recorded in other parts of the world.

Extreme waves are large spontaneous waves, sometimes known as 'rogue waves'. Some are thought to reach up to 30 metres high, and are probably the reason more than 200 supertankers and container ships have been lost during the past two decades. These huge walls of water, which the captain of the *Queen Elizabeth II* once described as like 'hitting the White Cliffs of Dover', were the stuff of legends until 2004, when, during a three-week period, a European Space Agency satellite detected ten extreme waves estimated to be more than 25 metres high at various places around the globe.

One stretch of water that is known for its rogue waves is the powerful Agulhas Current, which flows south-westwards along the coast of southern Africa. Here, oceanographers have discovered that ordinary waves encounter swirling eddies in the ocean, and concentrate the energy to form the much larger rogues.

The vortices are known as Agulhas Rings, the water circling at about the same speed as a person walks. They can be so big and powerful, up to 150 kilometres across, that some scientists have likened them to black holes in space. Once trapped in the gigantic whirlpool, even water cannot get out, and it can remain there for over a year. In the Southern Ocean, these rings are thought to be important in moving warm waters northwards, away from the Antarctic, and so counteract to some extent the impact of global warming on the region's ice sheets and glaciers. They are part of a global oceanic system that is akin to the circulatory system of the human body.

BIG WAVE SURFING (below)
German surfer Sebastian Steudtner rides a giant wave at Praia do Norte, Nazaré, Portugal.

One Ocean

Agulhas Rings from the Agulhas Current spill from the Indian Ocean into the South Atlantic. It shows how the world's five oceans – Pacific, Atlantic, Indian, Arctic and Southern – are not isolated bodies of water. They are interconnected, forming a single ocean, known as the World or Global Ocean. It transports energy, mainly in the form of heat and movement, and matter, as solids, dissolved substances, and gases, around the globe, a transport and circulatory system popularly known as the 'ocean conveyor belt'.

One leg of the circuit that has been intensely studied by oceanographers is in the North Atlantic. Here, warm surface waters are carried by the wind-driven Gulf Stream from the tropics towards the Arctic. Off the coasts of Greenland, intensely cold dry winds blow down from the ice-bound land surface; these winds evaporate the water, increasing the density in the ocean. The dense, cold water sinks into the deep sea, forming the North Atlantic

TRANS-OCEAN TRAVELLER (above) Leatherback turtles follow the Gulf Stream and other ocean currents of the North Atlantic Gyre between breeding beaches in tropical South America and jellyfish-rich feeding sites off the temperate coast of northwest Europe.

Deep Water current. This flows southwards at a depth of between 1,500 and 4,000 metres, until it mixes with similar waters from the Antarctic. It is then carried as Circumpolar Deep Water into the deep Indian and Pacific oceans.

On some coasts and around oceanic islands, the winds and local topography cause nutrient-rich waters from the deep sea to well up to the surface, so-called 'upwellings', and on other coasts the surface waters sink to the depths as 'downwellings'. Both have a profound effect on marine life, fuelling the food chain and influencing where animals live or migrate.

All this is an oversimplification, of course, but it shows how all the oceans and all parts of the oceans, at all depths, are linked, not only horizontally but also vertically. It's also clear to see that, with a changing climate, the warming Arctic Ocean is less likely to sink and feed the North Atlantic Deep Water current, so the entire conveyor belt would be slowed or could even come to a halt, with potentially disastrous consequences for weather and climates around the world.

'They wait for the larger boats to drop their nets. It acts like a dinner bell, and all the orcas in the area gather around. Quite a few herring slip from the nets, and this is what they are waiting for. They are very smart animals. They are not going to put in a big effort to feed during the day when they know that, at the end of the day, they will be provided with an easier meal... but feeding like this can be risky.'

Indeed, while the production team was on station, a drama unfolded. 'When the fishermen tried to haul in the net, the orcas panicked and a young orca was trapped inside,' Eve spotted. 'It was really fighting for its life. It was very painful to witness.'

Fortunately, Eve was able to persuade the fishermen to drop the net. 'We didn't believe that whale was going to make it. We thought it was going to die, but what was most impressive to see was the reaction of the family. It stayed around the boat until the end. It was a huge relief to see the orca finally get back to the sea.'

The orcas are intensely vocal animals. During carousel feeding, they call loudly to one another and, when the young whale was trapped, the family called to it constantly. Such commotion does not go unnoticed. Larger whales are listening. Humpback and fin whales have learned what the cacophony means and they suddenly appear, barging the hunting orcas aside. The gatecrashers lunge through the tight shoals of herring with mouths agape, engulfing the best part of the orcas' hard-won prey in a few enormous gulps.

'The humpback whales would often come in force,' recalls Jonathan, 'Five to ten abreast – that's a lot of whale!'

The humpbacks' arrival is a relatively new event, first noticed by the Norwegian scientists five or six years ago. The whales head for the Norwegian coast after spending the summer feeding around the Svalbard Archipelago in the Barents Sea. In late autumn, they stop off at the fjords for a final top-up on herring and may stay deep into winter, before continuing to breeding sites as far away as the Caribbean, a one-way journey of about three months. However, when they return, there is no guarantee that they will find the orcas in the same place. It seems every twenty years or so, the herring change their overwintering site.

HERRING SUPPER (right) Having swatted the corralled herring with their powerful tails, the orcas scoop up the dead and dying fish one at a time.

Arctic Mother

The islands of Svalbard, to the north of the Norwegian mainland, are popular with marine life in summer. Drawn by the superabundance of food at this time of year, the humpback and fin whales are joined by gigantic blue whales, along with belugas and several species of seals. Millions of seabirds – guillemots, little auks, puffins, razorbills, kittiwakes and fulmars – fill the cliff sides with seasonal colonies. But some Arctic animals are at a seasonal disadvantage, with much less ice than in winter on which to hunt or rest.

Walruses must haul their bulk onto beaches. Hundreds gather at the water's edge but, like any large gathering, their odour attracts unwelcome attention. Polar bears, like walruses, depend on the ice. It is where they hunt seals during the winter, so with little ice in summer, they head for Svalbard's beaches too. Downwind from the gathering, the bears quickly detect the presence of walruses, and from a considerable distance away, for they have an extraordinary sense of smell. When they plod onto the beach, they cause quite a stir.

WALRUS BEACH (below) An 'ugly' or 'huddle' of walruses gathers on a Svalbard beach. Most are males, but there are mothers with calves scattered about.

Bears have the advantage on land, so walruses will try to get back into the water to escape from them. Adult walruses can handle the situation. They can shake themselves free from a polar bear attack, their thick blubber protecting them from teeth and claws, but they still lose their nerve, especially females, for their youngsters are vulnerable, both from the bears and from being crushed by the panicking adults.

A mother in the midst of the fray tries to guide her pup towards the sea. They can both outswim a polar bear, and they put a good few metres between themselves and the beach. But once they are in the water, they cannot return to the beach whilst bears are present. They need to haul out onto an ice floe, but these are becoming fewer and farther between, due mainly to the warming climate.

The problem is that Svalbard has experienced the fastest and most profound loss of regional sea ice in recent years. In the Arctic during 2016, the summer was the warmest since records began. A combination of events caused the temperature to soar. A general warming of the Arctic, southerly winds pushing warm air from mid-latitudes, and an extreme El Niño warming event in the Pacific (one of the worst for decades) conspired to heat up the Arctic Ocean so the summer sea temperatures off the east and west coasts of Greenland were 5°C above the average for 1982–2010. In fact, in recent years, the Arctic is warming up at about twice the rate as the rest of the planet. This has caused what sea ice survives to thin. Until 1985, 45 per cent of the region had multiyear sea ice. Almost half the sea ice did not melt in summer, so in subsequent years the ice layers built up. Now only 22 per cent is thick multiyear ice, the rest being thin first-year ice, and a walrus mother with pup needs the thick stuff.

A slab of ice from a nearby glacier would do the trick, but competition for the ice is fierce and walrus mothers are not keen to share. It is some time before the pair finds a vacant slab of ice. Following their fate were Jonathan Smith and cameraman Ted Gifford, and it was difficult for them not to become emotionally involved.

PROTECTIVE MOTHER (below) If danger threatens, mothers with vulnerable calves seek the safety of the sea. They can out-swim polar bears, one of their main predators.

'This was one of the most beautiful and tender moments that I have ever been lucky enough to see: an animal so often portrayed as monstrous showing that she is actually one of the most caring ...' JONATHAN SMITH, Producer

LIGHTS, CAMERA, ACTION! (above)
While in the sea, the walruses are more inquisitive than frightened by the presence of the film crew.

NO ROOM AT THE INN (overleaf)
A mother and calf are prevented from hauling out onto an ice floe by the incumbents. In a warming arctic, ice floe refuges are already at a premium.

'You try to disengage yourself from the drama playing out in front of you, but when the mother and pup finally made it to an ice floe, and the pup cuddled up to its mother, Ted and I could not help looking up from our monitors and letting out a sigh of relief.'

And they were in for another little surprise. The mother reassured her baby by 'whisker kissing'. 'This was one of the most beautiful and tender moments that I have ever been lucky enough to see: an animal so often portrayed as monstrous showing that she is actually one of the most caring mums in the entire animal kingdom. These moments were quite extraordinary. As their blubber is too thick to feel a normal touch, the walrus mother comforts her offspring by touching their sensitive whiskers – truly heart-warming.'

The young walrus is dependent on its mother for at least three more years and they are both reliant on the ice being there. Without the ice, they have nowhere safe to haul out and rest, and climate change and rising sea temperatures mean that summer sea ice may be a thing of the past. For now, the interconnecting currents of the single global ocean are still doing their job as part of the planet's life-support system, but for how much longer? There are challenging times ahead for the Arctic's wildlife, and, as you'll read in the following pages, for marine life all over the world.

chapter two
Coast

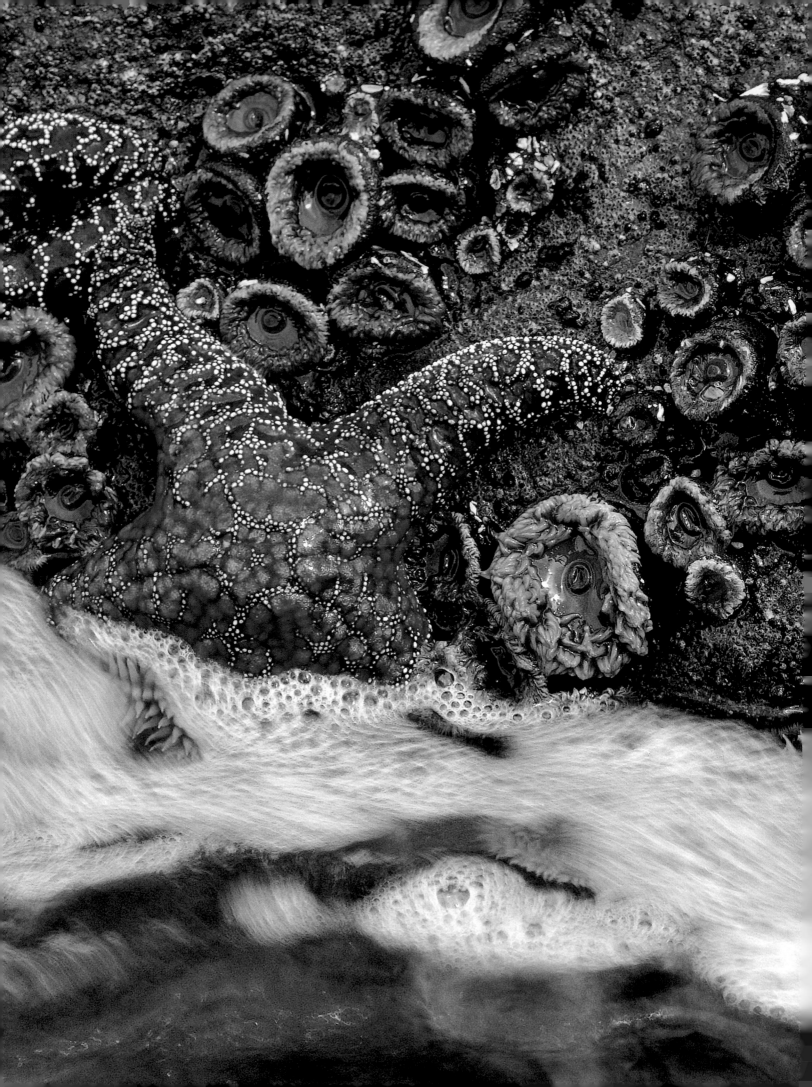

IN-BETWEEN WORLD (left) An ochre sea star is in danger of drying out as the tide recedes on a North Pacific shore.

SWASH AND BACKWASH (previous page) Waves erode shores and build beaches, while shore animals hang on or hide away.

The seashore can be many places – rocky shore, sandy spit, pebble beach, salt marsh, mudflat, estuary, fjord or sea cliff – but they all have one thing in common: they are places of constantly changing extremes. Life here is pounded by waves, fried by the sun, frozen by snow and ice, and swamped by freshwater. There are rapid swings of temperature, salinity and light intensity, with the constant danger of overheating, drying out or being washed away... and all of this in a single day.

Then there are people. Evidence is mounting that the first humans followed the coast and fed on marine life as they colonised the world. Today, coastal waters, more than any other part of the ocean, play host to countless millions of us, along with our recreational fads, unpleasant effluents and insidious pollution. All this is predicted to worsen as more energy enters the system, with a warming world and rising sea temperatures leading to a predicted increase in the number and intensity of powerful storms. This would destroy not only the coast's natural habitats but also places of human habitation.

Yet marine life thrives here. It is the sea's most productive zone, so the stakes are high and the rewards great, but they come at a price. Living organisms must have the ability to survive between two very different worlds. This is where the land meets the sea, the toughest place to live in

The Arrival

During the course of the day, dark, round shadows appear in the shallow inshore waters off beaches on the Pacific coast of Costa Rica. They are not inanimate rocks but living Olive Ridley sea turtles, and for several hours they sit motionless on the seabed, resting, maybe even asleep, conserving energy prior to a coming event that will require a herculean effort.

By early evening, they begin to stir. They swim parallel to the shore, their small heads bobbing above the surface to catch a breath, before submerging for five minutes or so at a time as if preparing for the big moment. Then, at some unknown signal, they start to emerge from the sea, changing from animals that are totally at home in the water to animals that are very uncomfortable on land.

At first, there are just twenty or thirty hauling their heavy bodies out of the surf, but gradually numbers increase until the beach resembles a moving conveyor belt of round, grey boulders. Many thousands of turtles will be crossing the beach and throughout the night they will just keep coming because they have to. Sea turtles are an ancient group of reptiles that are still bound to the land for this one vital purpose – to lay their eggs – so mothers must cross the frontier between land and sea and, for several exhausting hours, leave the confines of the ocean. It's a huge challenge, but despite the hardships, the rewards are worth it.

It is the rainy season on a dark night a few days before the three-quarter moon, and these female sea turtles have come to deposit their eggs in the black, volcanic sand. It is known locally as the *arribada* ('arrival'), and it is probably one of the most traumatic things a female sea turtle has to do during her life. More used to being supported by the water, her heavy body pushes down painfully on her internal organs, including her lungs. She wheezes and coughs, and glutinous tears ooze down from the corners of her eyes.

She sniffs at the sand, and when it is the right consistency and dampness she starts to dig. Using her spade-like hind limbs, she excavates a pit the shape of a teardrop. Manoeuvring her bulk over the

THE WAIT (opposite) Olive Ridley sea turtles are a solitary, open-ocean species. During the day, they wait just offshore, as if preparing for the transition from water to land.

ARRIBADA (below and overleaf) Thousands of female Olive Ridley sea turtles emerge from the ocean to deposit their eggs in the sand of a Costa Rican beach.

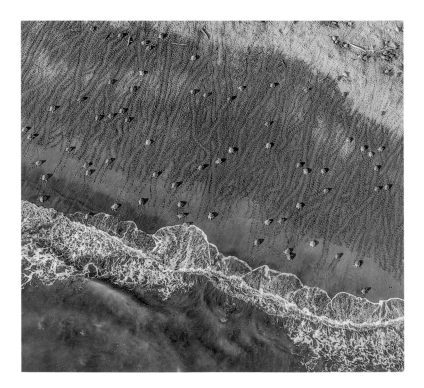

hollow, she lets out a huge sigh, and slowly and deliberately she deposits up to 100 eggs, each the size of a ping-pong ball. Then, using her front flippers, she covers them and, with one last gargantuan effort, hauls her body back to the sea.

If she was the only turtle on the beach, her clutch would be undisturbed and probably many of her embryos would develop successfully and later hatch out, but she is not alone. Thousands of other mothers are excavating the same stretch of sand, the late arrivals inadvertently digging up the eggs of the early birds. It is just what the egg thieves have been waiting for.

Black vultures, wood storks and great-tailed grackles are in the vanguard, and this is their moment. They squabble for the exposed nests, some even snatching the soft-shelled eggs at the very moment they are laid. Coatis, recognised by their erect, striped tails and long snouts, dig up buried eggs. Stray dogs and feral pigs join them, rooting around in the sand, yet there is plenty for all. During the course of a single *arribada* over several days, hundreds of thousands of females emerge from the sea, and they deposit tens of millions of eggs safely beyond the reach of the tide. With so many eggs, 'predator swamping' means that the thieves cannot eat them all, and nesting at night reduces the risk of nest predation. Some babies will have a chance to grow.

When the mothers go back to the sea, they all head off their separate ways. Olive Ridley sea turtles are more at home in the open ocean alone than on the shore with thousands of others of their own kind, but before they hit deep water they must run a gauntlet of sharks and American crocodiles from a nearby estuary. Even if they get past and survive, the fishing nets are another danger. In the past, thousands of turtles were caught in fine-meshed shrimp nets dragged by trawlers; many were drowned, and the population dwindled. Now local fishermen must by law have nets with turtle-excluder devices that enable the turtles to escape. It means a few more will return to join the next *arribada*.

Living Water Blasters

The Olive Ridley sea turtles are short-term visitors to the coast, but at Roebuck Bay on the west side of the Dampier Peninsula in Western Australia there are animals that take advantage of high tides over vast mud flats, rich in food. And, although they don't actually leave the sea, they do put their heads out of the water.

Red sand beaches, tidal creeks and mangroves border this remote, shallow bay. The mangroves are nursery sites where all kinds of young fish, crustaceans and molluscs hide during their formative years. Watching out for the careless or the overconfident are bluenose salmon and other hungry predators. Loose schools of fish patrol the edge of the mangroves in search of smaller fish, prawns and worms, but they too must watch their backs: although they have the benefit of living in murky water, there is a creature here that can find them, whatever the visibility.

The snubfin dolphin, or 'snubby' as it has become known, frequents river mouths and areas close to mangroves and seagrass beds in water less than 20 metres deep off coasts in the northern half of Australia. It is shy but gregarious, similar in shape to the closely related Irrawaddy dolphin of southern Asia. It was only classified as a separate species in 2005 and, as assistant producer Will Ridgeon discovered, it is notoriously difficult to find:

'The huge tides in the bay meant that visibility was almost zero, so it was impossible to know where the snubfins were going to pop up. Once we located them, though, we saw that when they weren't hunting they were incredibly social and playful.'

In the turbid waters, the snubby, like all dolphins, depends on echolocation to find its prey, which includes a variety of fishes, such as bluenose salmon, as well as crustaceans, octopus and squid. Snubbies sometimes root in the mud looking for crabs, but when fishing often raise their heads above water and look about – a behaviour known as spyhopping. And then they do something very unusual: they squirt a mouthful of water.

The water jet can reach several metres, and it is often used as a kind of 'tool' to surprise and disorientate its prey. The dolphin

WATER JET (below) An Australian snubfin dolphin squirts water to confuse its prey. It is behaviour unique to this species and its close relative the Irrawaddy dolphin.

AUSTRALIA'S OWN (above) Snubfins are shy, avoid boats, and are hard to see in the turbid waters of Roebuck Bay. Although not the most acrobatic of dolphins, they spyhop, lobtail, wave their flippers, and sometimes make low leaps from the water

can be very precise. It squirts the water just over the head of the fish so the disturbance is behind it. The fish immediately bolts, straight into the snubfin's open mouth. 'Some snubfin seemed to be more accomplished spitters than others,' Will noticed. 'It must be a real skill.'

Confirmation that spitting is used as a unique fishing strategy came when Will and the BBC film crew caught a dolphin in the act of swallowing a fish captured in this way. Previously, Australian scientists had observed spitting when dolphins were hunting, when fish schools were active, and often when birds were swooping for a prospect of something to eat. Until they had these pictures, however, they had never seen a direct capture.

For now, though, a serious concern is whether this behaviour will be seen for much longer. Like many species of coastal dolphins, the snubfin is vulnerable to the degradation of its habitat, the danger of drowning in fishing and anti-shark nets, ship strikes, and stress from underwater noise, which results in a diminished immune system and susceptibility to diseases, while beyond Australia fishermen still catch snubfins for food. In Roebuck Bay, where the BBC filmed, two out of three snubfins have been injured, probably by boat strikes and fishing gear. The total number living today is unclear, but best estimates indicate there are less than 10,000 mature individuals in the world, the majority living around the northern coasts of Australia.

Stuck Fast

On wild and windy shores, it is remarkable that any life can gain a hold on the slippery, wet rocks, but acorn barnacles and limpets do. They clamp tightly to the rock face. The acorn barnacle is a crustacean surrounded by circular plates with a top that opens when the tide is in and closes when it goes out, preventing it from drying out. It can live in the most exposed sites because it glues itself to the bare rock surface using special cement from a gland at the base of its antenna; in effect, it lies upside down with its legs in the air, fixed to the rock by its fforehead.

The limpet is a cone-shaped marine snail without any coiling of its shell. It has adhesive mucus, but also uses its powerfully muscular foot to fix it firmly to the rock by suction. Unlike the barnacle, the limpet can move around, although it always returns to exactly the same spot before the tide goes out. The little oval patch it leaves on the rock – known as a 'home scar' – is kept clear of algae for maximum adhesion. The limpet feeds with a radula or 'tongue' lined with teeth that scrape algae from rocks. The teeth are made from the strongest material known in nature, even stronger than spider silk, and have a tensile strength up to thirteen times that of human teeth.

Once in place, the limpet is extremely difficult to budge. The crushing claws of large lobsters can break into them and oystercatchers will try to prise them off, but the champion limpet-eater is South Africa's tadpole-shaped giant clingfish or rocksucker. Studying its every move has been filmmaker Craig Foster, a recognised field expert in marine biology, who has been diving in the same general area of False Bay everyday for the past six years in an attempt to better understand the creatures that live there. He has found that the clingfish gains an advantage over its competitors by hunting limpets in places too dangerous for other fish to go – in amongst huge waves and jagged rocks.

'To survive here, the clingfish uses a suction pad, formed by modified fins underneath its body,' Craig reveals. 'It's so powerful it can hold about 200 times the fish's bodyweight, and specialised hairs on the pad stop it sliding on the slippery algae-covered rocks. In between tides, it swims to the safety of its small cave and attaches itself upside-down on the roof. The suction pad helps it conserve energy, as the fish has no need to fight against the swirling currents.'

The clingfish hangs around in its cave for the tide to come in, and is often the first in the queue to have a go at the newly submerged limpets. This is where its other key feature comes in: very large and prominent front teeth. It was once thought that the fish used these to lever limpets away from the

SHELL TWISTER (opposite)
1-2 The giant clingfish eyes up a plump and juicy limpet that is attached firmly to the rocks. It grabs it in its mouth and, before the shellfish has time to clamp down…

3-4 … the fish twists its body through 90 degrees, breaks the limpet's suction, and pulls it away from the rocks.

underlying rock, but Craig has found that there is more to it than this:

'It was challenging to film the clingfish because it's a shy and cryptic creature, and it strikes its limpet prey in about one-third of a second. I filmed the fish over a period of one year at 240 frames per second, which slows down the action about ten times, and this revealed behaviour not noticed before.

'Prior to an attack, the clingfish goes through a shivering phase, its fins quivering and its body tensing up. It then grabs the limpet shell with its sharp teeth and twists through 90 degrees, much like we open a bottle cap. This twisting motion breaks the vacuum seal created by the limpet's foot. The fish juggles the limpet with its mouth, as it must position it upside-down to swallow, shell and all. While the soft parts are digested, the shells are stacked like interlocking hats in the stomach, covered in lubricating mucus and regurgitated as a single unit.'

X-ray pictures confirmed that the empty limpet shells are stacked in the fish's foregut, and Craig points out that clingfish in other parts of South Africa, particularly large individuals, might lever off limpets as was first thought, but all the clingfish in his study site in False Bay adopt the same twisting 'bottle-opening' method, another new discovery and a 'first' for television.

ROCKSUCKER (opposite) South Africa's giant clingfish or rocksucker is about 30 centimetres long, the largest member of the clingfish family.

STACKING PLATES (below left) Clingfish swallow the entire limpet, shell and all. The shells are regurgitated in a tidy stack, like plates in the kitchen.

'It was challenging to film the clingfish because it's a shy and cryptic creature, and it strikes its limpet prey in about one-third of a second.' CRAIG FOSTER, Biologist and Filmmaker

Rockpool Refuge

Life in this intertidal zone is usually severely challenged by the coming and going of the tides, especially during winter storms, but one place that relies on those tides is the rock pool. Every day it is flushed with fresh seawater, and when the tide goes out and the churning ceases, a few moments of calm descend on the pool. Its inhabitants begin to emerge from their hiding places. Sea stars and hermit crabs are often first out, followed by nudibranchs and small fish, and they all share a weakness. They may be located in the intertidal zone, but they have not yet thrown off the yoke of having to be fully immersed in seawater for all of their life.

The sea stars are trendsetters, and they can change the face of this humble pool. The eminent American ecologist Robert T. Paine studied them, and he found that mussel beds outside of rock pools survived well because the sea stars could only attack them for half the day; that is, at high tide. The mussels *in* rock pools could be consumed at all states of the tide, so there are fewer of them, leaving more space for other marine life. It led Paine to consider sea stars as 'keystone species', a term he introduced

SNEAKY HUNTER (below and opposite)
1 A sea star sidles up to a keyhole limpet, moving smoothly across the seabed on its hundreds of tiny tube feet. Those at the ends of its arms detect the odour of the limpet.

2 The sea star slides in for the kill, but is thwarted as the limpet pulls up its skirt. Its mantle repels the sea star.

3 If the sea star persists in its attack, a banded scaleworm pokes out its head and nips at the sea star's feet.

4 The limpet and the scaleworm live to fight another day, while the sea star smells out another victim.

1

2

to highlight animals that have a large impact on animal communities even though their numbers may be relatively small. They affect the lives of many other animals and therefore determine the types and numbers of other species present in the ecosystem.

The sea star travels about its domain on its hundreds of tube feet and those on the tips of its arms are sensitive to odours in the water and the promise of food. The keyhole limpet is a target, but this shellfish has secret defences tucked underneath its shell.

When the sea star makes contact, the limpet deploys a protective skirt. It rises off the underlying rock to twice its height and extends its mantle, normally hidden underneath, to cover both its shell and its foot. The probing sea star is unable to gain a hold on the mantle tissue, which appears to be slippery. However, if the sea star fails to back down, the limpet has a backup. Living under its shell is the banded scaleworm. Its jaws shoot out and nip at the sea star's tube feet, an effective way to get it to back off.

3

4

The Creature from the Rock Lagoon

Rock pools and their inhabitants depend on being recharged by the incoming tide, but there are creatures in this neighbourhood that came from the sea and have taken the bold step towards living on land. They view rock pools and the sea itself as potential death traps with lurking predators, and they steer clear of them. Having left the water, however, they are exposed to new dangers, such as predatory seabirds. To survive here, they have to be either well camouflaged against the rocks and seaweeds or light on their feet.

The brightly coloured Sally Lightfoot crab adopts the second strategy, making the move successfully from ocean to land, yet is still dependent

SALLY LIGHTFOOT (below) These colourful crabs live on the rocks of windy shores, where they feed mainly on algae. They are extremely nimble and almost impossible to catch, except, that is, if you are a cunning moray eel or octopus.

on the sea. It lives and feeds just out of reach of sea spray in the intertidal zone but it needs water to reproduce. The mother carries her eggs until they hatch, but then places them carefully in the sea, where they are washed out to the open ocean to complete their development.

The crab is said to get its name from a Caribbean dancer, in reference to the way it jumps deftly from rock to rock and over pools. It is quick moving and difficult to catch, so predators must have a few tricks up their sleeves if they want to bag one, as producer Miles Barton discovered. Brazilian ecologist and filmmaker João Paulo Krajewski invited him to an oceanic island in the Fernando de Noronha Archipelago off the eastern tip of Brazil, where a colourful scene greeted Miles and his crew:

'The Sally Lightfoot crabs are simply spectacular: a red and yellow wave of crabs walking along the tideline. They feed on freshly exposed algae, and are careful not to fall into the water. They seem to have a positive dislike of it. Sometimes, though, they are caught out by the incoming tide and marooned on rocks and forced to swim for it. In a complete panic, they scuttle across the water, their legs paddling frantically. They do this because there are moray eels here, and these eels like crabs.'

The eels adopt one of two stalk-and-attack strategies. Some follow the tide in and intercept crabs on their temporary islets, while others hide in rock pools waiting for crabs to pass by. As a consequence, the crabs are very careful when approaching a pool. They move slowly and deliberately, lest they attract attention, for the moray eel is alert to sudden movements.

The species here is the chain moray eel, and it differs significantly from other moray eels. Its bluntly pointed teeth, some almost molar-like, are ideal for catching and crushing crabs. It hunts by stalking its target,

EEL AMBUSH (above) Chain moray eels are about 45 centimetres long on average, but can be up to 65 centimetres. They leave the water in pursuit of crabs, and can be high and dry on the rocks for up to 30 minutes.

CRAB CATCHER (above) Chain moray eels are one of a handful of crustacean-eating moray eels with crushing teeth, rather than the sharp, fish-catching teeth of most other morays.

watching its every move, predicting where will be the best place to set an ambush, and like a snake, it thrusts its head out of the water and grabs its victim.

Slithering over the very slippery rocks, Will Ridgeon, working with cameraman Dan Beecham, was hard pressed to be in the right place at the right time.

'Trying to predict when and where the moray eel was going to strike was a real challenge. It was a case of following an eel that appeared to be hunting and try to second-guess the crab it was after. The moray strikes were lightning fast, and a lot of crabs had battle wounds from these violent encounters but, to secure a meal, the moray had to grab the crab's carapace. If it seized a limb, the crab would jettison the leg and get away.'

In this way, smaller crabs are crushed and swallowed whole, while larger crabs usually lose a leg rather than their life – they can grow a new one, after all.

'**Trying to predict when and where the moray eel was going to strike was a real challenge. It was a case of following an eel that appeared to be hunting and try to second-guess the crab it was after.**' WILL RIDGEON, Assistant Producer, 'Coast' and 'The Deep'

If the eel fails to catch the crab, it will sometimes slither over the rocks and set up an ambush in a neighbouring pool, momentarily becoming a terrestrial predator. But if it encounters its prey while out of the water, the crab inevitably gets away. On land, the eel is no match for the nimble Sally Lightfoot crab.

On the same stretch of shore, young octopuses have also been seen to leap from the water remarkably quickly and snatch crabs from the rocks. They drag them below the surface, enveloping them in the webbing between their arms and dismembering them with their strong parrot-like beak. Will had to watch where he put his feet. 'The octopuses were surprisingly aggressive. They jumped out at us as we walked past.'

'But they were a real bonus,' added Miles. 'They were commoner than the eels and their ambush spots were more predictable, so we ended up with two predators for the price of one.

SOLITARY WORK (above) On an enchanted island in the Fernando de Noronha Archipelago, a UNESCO World Heritage Site, wildlife cameraman Rod Clarke waits patiently for the crabs to be active and for the eels to go hunting.

ABOVE THE SPRAY ZONE (opposite) Sally Lightfoot crabs get as close as they can to the water in order to feed on the freshest algae. If a large wave crashes in, they flatten their bodies against the rock and grip tightly with their powerful legs.

Fish out of Water

Few modern fish have made the transition from sea to land, but there are some. The chain moray eel can withstand up to 30 minutes out of water when setting up its ambush, and mudskippers use their fins to 'skip' across the mud, defending territories amongst the mangroves and courting the opposite sex while the tide is out. However, the fish that takes terrestrial living to new heights is the Pacific leaping blenny in Micronesia. It spends its entire adult life out of the water in the splash and intertidal zones.

This 8-centimetre-long blenny is beautifully camouflaged, blending in with the algae-covered rocks and therefore hidden from the prying eyes of birds, crabs and lizards, all potential predators. It feeds on the slime, using its teeth to scrape it from the rocks, and has a preference for algae freshly exposed by the outgoing tide. The fish are most active for up to 4 hours at mid-tide, mainly during the day when it is not too hot. At high tide, with waves crashing against the shore, they cling to rocks or hide in crevices, and at low water they retreat into damp corners to retain moisture, but at mid-tide groups of blennies might line up at the edge of the sea like children dodging the waves ready to feed, and they have a unique way of getting about.

If a predator should detect them or a large wave disturb them, they can leap out of the way to higher ground – hence their common name. The secret is in the tail. It can be twisted through 90 degrees, enabling the fish to propel itself with considerable agility from one place to another. Only then, Miles Barton discovered, do they reveal where they are.

'At first sight, the blennies are so well camouflaged that they are almost invisible against the brown rocks. It's only when a wave comes in that you see the flashes of silver, as the sun reflects off their bodies. If you watch really closely, you can see how they flatten their oar-like tails and push them against the rock to propel themselves into the air.'

The movement of the tail also enables them to leap from one hollow to the next in order to find a partner. This fish is so well adapted to the terrestrial lifestyle that it socialises, courts and lays its eggs on land.

At mid-tide, females feed for longer than males, and if another blenny should approach within 20 centimetres, they signal aggressively by flashing their red dorsal fin and changing their skin colour to black, the heightened aggression linked to competition for food. This is only tempered when many females huddle together in a rock shelter during high and low water.

Males tend to avoid other males, and they are territorial. Should two meet, they use the same signal, although the intensity of colour in a male's

FLASH A FIN (opposite top left) The male leaping blenny advertises his availability to females by showing off his brightly coloured dorsal fin.

ROCK NEST (opposite top right) This male has a large nest hollow amongst the rocks, and attracts the most females. He'll guard the eggs, but the larvae develop at sea before returning to the land.

LANDLUBBER (opposite bottom) The leaping blenny feeds on the algae it scrapes from the rocks. Its unusual lifestyle out of water has led scientists to consider it a terrestrial species.

Seabird Cities

At breeding time, seabirds occupy the next coastal zone inland – the land itself. Towering above the rocks of the splash and intertidal zones are sea cliffs, the nesting sites of puffins, guillemots and other seabirds. They spend most of their lives at sea, where they dive below the waves and with stubby wings almost 'fly' underwater in pursuit of fish and squid, but at breeding time they must leave the sea and return to the land. Puffins dig tunnels or take over rabbit burrows on cliff tops and guillemots occupy ledges further down. They often form breeding colonies containing thousands of birds.

During the long days of the brief Arctic summer, the small island of Hornøya in the Barents Sea, the most easterly point in Norway, is host to more than 15,000 common guillemots and 7,800 Atlantic puffins, and they are joined on the cliffs by kittiwakes, razorbills, and shags. Nesting nearby are colonies of herring gulls and isolated pairs of great black-backed gulls.

Seabird researchers are at odds over why seabirds gather together in such large numbers. Some say that it is a case of 'predator swamping': with so many eggs and chicks, predators are quickly sated. There are also more birds to mount a defence, and large numbers of seabirds swirling about in the air will probably confuse potential attackers. On the other hand, seabird colonies are extremely noisy, unbelievably smelly and very conspicuous from a considerable distance. They are likely to attract unwelcome attention, making the birds and their offspring vulnerable. There are benefits, though.

Birds on the cliffs watch those returning from fishing excursions, checking out those carrying small fish in their bills. They give away the direction of the best feeding grounds so the watchers head out in the right direction to fish for themselves. The city has become an information centre where birds take advantage of collective knowledge, but the constant underlying threat from aerial predators means that simply flying in and out can be fraught with dangers.

Pirate-like Arctic skuas chase and harass returning birds until they regurgitate or drop their hard-won catch, and then wolf it down themselves. This can be a serious setback for the nesting birds for they may have made a round trip of more than 100 kilometres. They must travel this great distance each day for two disturbing reasons.

Fishermen have exhausted the nearshore feeding sites that once offered a steady supply of fish on the doorstep, and climate change and the warming of the ocean have affected the distribution of the zooplankton which feed two important prey species – sand eels and capelin. They have

OVERCROWDED (above) On this cliff face on Hornøya, almost every ledge is occupied by pairs of nesting guillemots.

all moved to cooler waters to the northeast, so the birds have had to fly increasingly further out to sea. If they lose food to skuas, it is more than an inconvenience; it is vital time wasted and chicks go hungry. This is just one of a series of compromises that seabirds make when nesting in such inaccessible places.

Balanced as they are on narrow ledges, the new generation of guillemots has had to face hazards from day one, but there are a few features that help keep many healthy. If rain falls on guillemot eggs, it forms droplets rather than running off, making the eggs water-repellent and self-cleaning. Eggs generally do not fall from the ledge, but parents sometimes knock them off when landing or taking off. Hatchlings are equally vulnerable. They must ensure they do not inadvertently slip off the edge and, at little more than 20 days old, the young guillemots must leap from their cliff. Miles Barton and cameraman Barrie Britton were there on the one special evening of the year when all the chicks are ready to jump.

'They can't fly at this stage,' Miles observed. 'They flap their tiny but rather useless wings to try to control their plummet. The cliffs were raining chicks, with anxious parents following them down. They plopped all around us, on the rocks and the lucky ones on the vegetation. The air filled with the calls of frantic parents and lost chicks. Over the space of a few hours, thousands of chicks must have jumped. It was one way to avoid being eaten. A couple of greater black-backed gulls had already eaten their fill and ignored the rest of the little balls of fluff clambering over the rocks towards the sea, but the drama was not over. These tiny birds then had to leap into the foaming waves that were crashing against the rocks. It was truly a magical evening we'll never forget.'

The chicks are able to dive immediately they hit the water, and they are fed by the father for a couple of months before they are on their own and have to fend for themselves, but where they end up has puzzled Tone Kristin Reiertsen, of the Norwegian Institute for Nature Research, who has been studying the birds for several years.

'During the whole winter, all the guillemots from Hornøya stay in the south-eastern Barents Sea, which is quite amazing because of the winter darkness and harsh conditions. They also dive to extreme depths, down to 180 metres, but only in midwinter. How they manage is a mystery.'

Producing more questions than answers, some of the time, what this research is showing is that guillemots are extraordinary survivors. In the course of a few weeks, the young birds have started out as terrestrial animals, switched to being aquatic, taken to the air, and then become exceptionally deep divers, a remarkable achievement for a ball of feathers weighing no more than a hamster when it leaves the nest.

FLYING UNDERWATER (above) Guillemots appear to swim underwater just as well as they can fly in the air, using their wings for propulsion. They hunt for small shoaling fish such as sand eels, capelin and sand lances, sometimes diving down to 180 metres and remaining below for a couple of minutes.

NATURE'S CLOWN (opposite) The Atlantic puffin, like the guillemot, must run the gauntlet of Arctic skuas when returning to the nest with its catch.

Trapped!

In the Galápagos Archipelago in the eastern Pacific, an equally intriguing story is unfolding, in which the land itself is to play a key role. The action takes place at the bottom of Wolf Volcano at the northern end of the island of Isabela, where the local hawks, herons and seabirds are watching their neighbours – a colony of Galápagos sea lions – for something quite extraordinary is about to happen.

Sea lions are at home on land and at sea, and they use this ability to operate in the two very different worlds to turn events to their advantage, and a gang of these sea lions is going fishing, not for mackerel or other small fish but huge yellowfin tuna – the species you are most likely to find on your plate.

The average yellowfin can weigh in at 60 kilograms, so it's not puny, and its swimming muscles, which are kept warmer than the surrounding seawater, can propel the super-sleek fish to speeds of 40 mph. With that

FISH SUPPER (opposite) A Galápagos sea lion feeds on a yellowfin tuna, while a heron watches and waits for scraps.

CLOSING IN (below) The sea lions herd the tuna into the shallow confines of a narrow bay, where the fish cannot escape. In this way, the larger-brained sea lions can outwit the faster tuna.

kind of power, it can outswim and outmanoeuvre most large marine predators, but when schools of tuna approach close to Isabela, attracted in by shoals of baitfish, they are in for a shock.

Galápagos sea lions are no slouches themselves. Bulls can be 2.5 metres long and weigh 360 kilograms, and they are fast and agile in the water, but for speed they are no match for a large tuna. They do, however, have a bigger and more complex brain than the fish, and they use it.

Fishermen first spotted the sea lions' extraordinary behaviour in 2014, and the BBC film crew has been the first to film it. They couldn't believe their eyes. As the school of tuna approaches the island, the sea lions swim out and start to drive the fish towards the shore. They choose a bay that gradually narrows, so the fish are entering a trap. Assistant producer Rachel Butler watched events unfold:

'The topography of the bay shows why the sea lions have chosen this particular spot. The volcanic lava forms a labyrinth of small bays that are linked to a deep channel running from the open ocean to the "killing beach". We called it "the broccoli", and when we saw the sea lions gaining speed and porpoising near the opening to the channel, we knew the hunt was on.

'Strategically, there was one sea lion who instigated the hunt, and if, say, fog obscured the early stages of the hunt, we could still hear them calling to each other, like soccer players on a football field. At first we thought the behaviour was random, each sea lion hunting when it was hungry, but it was not until we got a drone in the air that their game plan became evident.

'There was always a "driver", often a big male we called "Mr Grey", and you'd see another sea lion peel off and block the deepest channel, keeping the tuna in the shallows. The smaller sea lions would then flank the

COUP DE GRÂCE (left) The fish is subdued by a powerful bite to the head.

Blubber Wall

While the tuna around the Galápagos Islands have sea lions and sharks to contend with, on an island in the South Atlantic a large and charismatic seabird has an even more formidable gauntlet to run or, at least, waddle.

Backed by snow-capped mountains, the broad sweep of the beach and hinterland at St Andrews Bay on South Georgia is often a seething mass of penguins. About 150,000 pairs nest here, one of the largest breeding colonies of king penguins in the world. Standing close to 1 metre tall, they are the second largest species of living penguins (the emperor is 10 centimetres taller), males a touch larger than the females.

Each pair has a single egg, which is laid between November and April, but, because chicks take 13 to 16 months to fledge, at any one time

TREAD GENTLY (below) The returning king penguins are very careful not to disturb the biggest and most powerful of the elephant seals – 'beachmaster'.

some pairs may be approaching the end of their breeding period with a 12-month-old chick, while other parents have only just started to incubate their egg. Both parents are on duty, round the clock for the first three weeks, and then every two or three days as they head out to sea to hunt. Older chicks tend to gather in large crèches while their parents are at sea. Even though each bird is enveloped in a dark brown, downy coat, fiercely cold katabatic squalls can blow down from nearby glaciers, so the youngsters huddle together to help keep warm.

On land king penguins are slow movers but in the sea they are transformed into sleek, fast-swimming predators. During the day, they dive generally to about 100 metres and remain submerged for about 5 minutes, although the current record holder was down for 9.2 minutes and dived to 343 metres. At night, they need go no more than 30 metres. This

is because their prey, mainly lanternfish and squid, are part of the daily vertical migration of marine life that rises towards the surface at night and hides in the deep sea by day. They rely less on swarms of krill than most other Southern Ocean predators.

The birds return to the bay fully laden with food, ready to regurgitate this natural and nutritious bouillabaisse to their chick, but as they emerge from the water a wall of blubber confronts them. Thousands of southern elephant seals, about half the world's population, have hauled out onto the beach, a living barrier between the penguin parents and the many thousands of chicks eagerly waiting on the other side.

The birds appear to almost tiptoe through the sprawling bodies, careful not to wake a snoozing beachmaster. These bulls are the real 'kings' around here, each dominant male surrounded by his harem of smaller females. If one should stir, a penguin might easily be squashed under an animal that weighs up to 4 tonnes and has a length of nearly 7 metres, the vital statistics of the heaviest and longest southern elephant seal ever known, a South Georgia resident and, in his time, the largest pinniped on Earth.

Having negotiated the elephant seal labyrinth, most parents try to locate their offspring, but, at some point, their parenting duties done, the adults return from the sea and bypass the crèches, walking inland to moult. Hundreds of birds just stand around, losing and growing new feathers at the same time. They discard and regrow four layers of deep insulation to renew their survival suits, but they must pay the price of not hunting and feeding: they lose at least 2 kilograms of bodyweight. They look terrible, dishevelled and forlorn, and it is important that they complete their moult as quickly as possible or there is the ever-present danger of freezing to death.

The fledging youngsters, meanwhile, take their first tentative steps into the sea, and, once in the water, they must be able to swim fast. Leopard seals, killer whales, and bull fur seals could be patrolling inshore waters. Sub-Antarctic islands in the South Atlantic are unforgiving places.

PATCHWORK OF PENGUINS (right) Adult king penguins form the patches of black and white, while youngsters show up as smudges of brown.

Shark Junction

It is mid-February at Palm Beach, Florida, and the sea is warm – about 23°C. Tourists escaping the winter weather flock here to bathe and soak up the sun. Little do they know, however, that just 100 metres from the shore they share the water with ten thousand sharks, taking a break from their annual migration. There are so many blacktip and spinner sharks gathered together that you could throw a stone and almost guarantee hitting one. It is one of the largest aggregations of sharks on the planet. They come from further south and congregate here before moving northwards. There are rich pickings at their destinations all along the Atlantic coast, and the bays and estuaries are known breeding grounds, but they appear to wait for the water temperature to rise at those more northerly sites – usually by about Easter – before continuing their journey north. This mass hesitation, however, is an opportunity to refuel with what is available locally.

Spinners and blacktips are enthusiastic hunters, but they do have a clumsy side. Large gangs chase dense shoals of bluefish and mullet, sometimes into very shallow water, the sea erupting in a feeding frenzy of thrashing sharks. A few even beach themselves, frantically squirming their way back into the water before the tide leaves them high and dry.

SHARK SCHOOL (above) During January and February each year, thousands of blacktip and spinner sharks come to within a few metres of beaches in southern Florida.

THE OPPORTUNIST (overleaf) The great hammerhead shark hunts spinner and blacktip sharks. It deliberately follows their migration, picking off stragglers.

Unsurprisingly, this enormous aggregation attracts unwelcome attention. Even medium-sized sharks have their predators, and their nemesis is a brute of a shark – the great hammerhead. It's up to 6 metres long and instantly recognised by its tall sickle-shaped dorsal fin, yet this enormous apex predator slides into the shallows to bag a meal, something these sharks have been doing since long before people built their villas and condominiums here.

It is these condominiums, however, that could put paid to natural spectacles like this. More than any place in the ocean, coastlines, which are more usually shaped by natural geological processes, are being destroyed by our desire to have a place by the sea. Concrete jetties, groins and sea walls keep the waves at bay. They might protect one community from inundation, but, because natural processes of erosion and deposition have been compromised, its neighbour down current is exposed to even worse erosion, so even more concrete has to be used. And the more the coast is hardened in this way, the less likely any marine life will exist or even visit here. The coast, far from being a dynamic and challenging environment for wildlife, is becoming an ecological desert, and this is occurring on coasts all over the world.

chapter three
Coral Reef

FLASH OF COLOUR (left) The tropical coral reef is a vibrant city with a host of colourful citizens under the sea.

DELICATE CORALS (previous page) Tropical coral reefs grow in warm, shallow seas in which the ambient water temperature is critical if the reef is to survive.

The tropical coral reef is a cosmopolitan city under the sea. There are high-rise blocks, narrow alleyways, broad avenues and grand piazzas, with diverse city dwellers from every major animal group on Earth. These reefs cover just 0.1 per cent of the ocean's surface area, yet they are home to 25 per cent of all known marine species, and new ones are being discovered every day. Surprisingly, tropical reefs are located in parts of the ocean where the water is poor in nutrients. Almost everything they need is manufactured within the city, and so the competition for space and resources is intense.

Some of these reefs are colossal structures – the Great Barrier Reef is so big it is clearly visible from space – but they are extremely delicate. Their health is dependent on clean, clear water, an abundance of sunlight, and a common water temperature of 25–30°C, so they are found only in shallow waters, away from major rivers, in a narrow band either side of the Equator bounded by latitudes 30°N and 30°S. These picky demands mean that tropical coral reefs are highly vulnerable to even minor glitches in the environment. They are like cities under siege. The impact of large-scale change, such as overfishing, ocean acidification and rising temperatures and sea levels, is potentially devastating.

RAINBOW REEFS (left and right) Corals fluoresce in all kinds of colours. The fluorescent colours can act as sun blocks that protect the resident zooxanthellae in the tissues of shallow water corals from the harmful rays of the sun. Deeper corals also fluoresce, not as a sunscreen, but to create additional light for zooxanthellae. Fluorescence can indicate whether a reef is healthy.

TUBE-DWELLER (bottom far right) Tube-dwelling anemones resemble sea anemones, but they lie buried in soft sediment and can pull back into a tube. They have two whorls of tentacles, an outer whorl of large tentacles that capture food and an inner whorl of small ones that manipulate it.

Dawn's Watery Chorus

The sun pushes up above the horizon. The ocean is calm. Seabirds break their nocturnal silence with a round of raucous calls, a strident welcome to the new day. In rainforests, fields and marshlands all over the world, birds join in with the dawn chorus, but the remarkable thing is that this daily performance is not confined to animals living above the waves. Below the surface, a cacophony of sounds fills the sea, the discordant voices of the 'choral reef'.

Just like songbirds on land in spring, the coral reef community lets rip at dawn and again at dusk, the sounds louder in the evening than in the morning, with the greatest intensity at the time of the new moon and lowest during the full moon. It coincides with times of greatest activity on the reef and whatever the time of day or year, it is an exuberant chorus created by some of the most unlikely performers. That fish make sounds has been known since the time of Aristotle in 350 BCE, but who would have thought sea urchins and shrimps were part of the choir?

The quietest sounds are the scrapes of sea urchin teeth as they feed, and a faint rasping sound of spines rubbing together, probably when cleaning. The globular shell or 'test' of the urchin amplifies the sound. The loudest sounds, often drowning out all others, are from snapping or pistol shrimps and, when many are snapping together, it sounds like bacon sizzling in a frying pan. The shrimp makes its sound, together with a bright flash of light, by shooting a cavitation bubble from the larger of its two claws. It creates an implosion that is so loud and has so much energy that the shockwave can knock out small fish, but it is more generally used to communicate with other snapping shrimps.

Compared to the shrimps, fish are a little more reserved, but what they lack in volume they make up for in variety. The black jewfish sounds like a foghorn, clownfish clack their jaws together, and, when stressed, the three-spined toadfish cries like a baby, one of the few fish known to make bi-phonic calls, a trick usually attributed to birds.

The coral reef's damselfish are especially chatty. They make popping sounds with their teeth and emit chirps by vibrating muscles against their swim bladder, and, from time to time, they invent new sounds. In recent years, the ubiquitous Ambon damselfish, from the Indo-Pacific region, was discovered to emit what the researchers have described as a 'wiping sound', because it sounds like a windscreen wiper on dry glass. Others have likened it to a dove cooing, but whatever the description, it is very different from the pops and chirps damselfish normally make. Competition is so fierce on the coral reef that the invention of a new sound is a good way to be heard above the grunts, grumbles, growls, thumps, drums, clicks and burps from the rest of the reef fishes.

RAUCOUS REEF (above) The noisy coral reef is a far cry from Jacque-Yves Cousteau's *Silent World*.

NEW SIGNAL (right) The Ambon damselfish produces chirps and pops, as well as a newly discovered sound scientists have called the 'wiping sound'.

Sounds heard throughout the year, such as the chomp of the parrotfish or the daytime grumble of the damselfish, are thought to be linked to feeding and defence of territory. For two to three months each year, however, these are drowned out by the cacophony of fish engaged in courtship and spawning events or in contests for local dominance between males.

Just like birds, female bicolour damselfish can tell apart the chirps of individual males, and males can identify the chirp of their nearest rival, distinguishing it from more distant males. Each morning, as they emerge from the safety of their nocturnal hiding holes, male damselfish must re-stake their claim on a small patch of real estate. Calling to each other ensures they are suitably spaced to avoid unnecessary fighting. Even so, on the reef in the early morning, some of its inhabitants do quarrel, and it can get physical. While the fish and shrimps are exchanging audible brickbats, the local sea turtles are just waking up and getting ready to do battle.

Turtle Rock Health Spa

In any great city, the morning rush hour sees commuters racing to their destinations, and the coral reef metropolis is no exception. Time wasted is feeding time lost, but for some the first appointment of the day is a visit to the health spa.

An old female green sea turtle emerges from the coral overhang under which she has spent most of the night asleep, lodged firmly in place to prevent her from floating up to the surface between breaths. While inactive she can hold her breath for several hours, but now it is time to move, and move fast. She wants to be first at the spa, and for the moment there's not another turtle in sight.

A sea turtle with algae covering its carapace and parasites on the softer parts of its body is going to be slower, less healthy and at a disadvantage compared to one without, so she heads for the wash-and-brush-up service provided by local cleaner fish. It would have been better to saunter. The disturbance has woken other turtles, and they've noticed she's making a break for it. There is only room for one turtle at a time at the spa, so the race is on.

On the reef at Sipadan, off the coast of Malaysian Borneo, Turtle Rock is a world-famous cleaning station. It is an unusual undersea landmark

LATE ARRIVALS (above) On one occasion, the film crew had to wait for over four hours for the turtles to turn up and settle into the cleaning station, and all for a 20-second shot!

TURTLE ROCK (opposite) Normally docile green sea turtles become very aggressive towards competitors for access to this often used cleaning station.

because the rocky outcrop has a well-worn hollow in the top that has been eroded by countless generations of sea turtles checking in to be cleaned. The first to arrive receives the five-star treatment, so the queue can involve a bit of argy-bargy, as underwater cameraman Roger Munns found out:

'Green turtles have a well-deserved reputation for being very docile, but they are not so friendly when they want their shells cleaned at Turtle Rock. They bite and headbutt each other in order to get the best spot. They're very aggressive.'

When the other turtles catch up and crowd in, they bite the lead female's flippers and generally make life difficult for her, but it's all to no avail: the first in is the first to be spruced up. Bicolour blennies appear from their burrows in the coral, and dark surgeonfish hover expectantly, ready to service the first customer of the day. The blennies deal with the parasites and dead skin, while the surgeonfish nibble on the algae covering the turtle's shell. With this arrangement, the fish get an easy meal and the turtle a smoother shell and clean skin, the symbiotic relationship between them known as 'mutualism', meaning both parties benefit. It's another way for them both to gain an advantage in the city.

Self-Medicating Dolphins?

Off the Egyptian coast, in the northern Red Sea, Indo-Pacific bottlenose dolphins have set up their own health club. The dolphins depend on the reef for shelter and protection from sharks, but also for their general wellbeing. During their daily ablutions the dolphins rub their bodies on sand, pebbles, seagrass and corals, and the ways in which they use them are not random.

They rub their entire body in sand, seagrass and gorgonian corals, but rub particular body parts on specific corals and sponges. It's thought they use leather corals and sponges for the head, underside and tail flukes, while they rub the edges of their pectoral fins on very hard corals. It is now known that some gorgonian corals (sea fans and sea whips) and certain sponges possess antibacterial and anti-fungal properties, so the dolphins may be using the coral to cleanse themselves, and to keep their skin free from disease and parasites – a form of self-medication. This highlights why some scientists think coral reefs could become the medicine cabinets of the twenty-first century.

Adult corals, along with the sponges that grow amongst them, are sessile animals fixed firmly to the seabed and, because they cannot run away, they need chemical defences to protect themselves. Those chemicals might also protect us. Already, antiviral, anti-cancer and anti-inflammatory agents have been isolated from sponges on Caribbean reefs. It is extraordinary to think that animals like dolphins may have been exploiting the medicinal properties of corals long before we even thought to look beneath the waves. These complex behaviours, however, are not confined to large-brained cetaceans.

DOCTOR DOLPHIN (below) The dolphin pod at Hurghada.

HEALTH CLUB (opposite)
1 A queue forms for the choice corals.
2 The edges of the fins are rubbed against hard corals.
3 Almost all of the body is treated in this way.
4 The tail flukes are the last to be treated.

Smart Fish

By sunup, the orange dotted tuskfish has already arrived at his workshop on Australia's Great Barrier Reef, and to get ahead in this challenging world it has opted for ingenuity. It has joined the exclusive club of animals – predominantly mammals and birds – that have found ways of using 'tools'. It likes to eat clams, so it uses a neat trick to expose one buried in the sand. Instead of blowing a mouthful of water at it, the fish turns away from the clam and snaps shut its gill covers, blasting water in the same way that closing a book creates a waft of air. Then it grabs the clam in its mouth and, with a deft movement of the head and body, smashes it against a coral. The blows are so precise that, after a short time, the shell breaks apart. The fish then gobbles it down, swallowing the soft flesh and spitting out shattered shell fragments.

While scouring the reef for signs of tuskfish activity, one individual in particular caught the eye of assistant producer Rachel Butler and underwater cameraman Roger Munns.

'We weren't really sure we were going to see anything when we first found the tuskfish we nicknamed "Percy", but within a few minutes he'd found a shell and set off to his favourite coral head, where he proceeded, with violent swings of his head, to smash it to bits. Although we knew what to expect, Rachel and I were both dumbfounded at his amazing behaviour.'

PERCY'S CASTLE (below) The tuskfish has an anvil in a porites coral, where he returns repeatedly to smash clams. The coral started to bleach in 2016, but the castle has since recovered.

TOOL USER (above) Percy the tuskfish travels far and wide each day to collect clams, which he diligently takes back to the same spot to crack open.

'Seeing a fish use a "tool" for the first time was truly remarkable,' adds Rachel. 'Percy came back to his "castle" each day. He was a tenacious little thing, swimming for hours every day in search of clams that he would bash on his anvil for up to 20 minutes at a time.'

Piles of broken shells scattered around the coral head indicate that the tuskfish regularly uses the same 'anvil'. Furthermore, similar collections of broken shells can be observed across the Great Barrier Reef, suggesting the behaviour may be widespread. Despite being a relatively conspicuous behaviour, anvil use in tuskfish had rarely been observed in Australia prior to commencement of filming *Blue Planet II* and has been professionally filmed for the first time by this series.

These resourceful tuskfish are in the wrasse family, and since these observations were reported several others have come to light. Off the Florida coast, the yellow-headed wrasse smashes scallops against an anvil rock, and in the Red Sea three species of wrasse collect sea urchins, drag them back to their territory, and break off the spines and split the test against a chosen rock to get at the soft parts inside.

Fish are not noted generally for their intelligence, but digging up a clam or collecting a sea urchin, carrying it some distance in its mouth to a preferred anvil and then smashing it open, like a sea otter, requires some degree of forward thinking, and for a fish that's a big deal.

Rag-and-Bone Fish

The charismatic clownfish shows enterprise too. It avoids the morning rush by working from home, usually under the protection of the stinging tentacles of a large sea anemone. Unlike many reef fishes that cast tiny eggs and sperm into the sea, the clownfish is a nest-builder, caring for a few large eggs that are laid carefully upon something hard, such as coral or rock, but this is not always easy to find. If the host anemone has planted itself in soft sand, it presents the fish with a problem, and one that requires an ingenious solution.

When it is time to spawn, the male clownfish leaves the safety of its home and enters the hustle and bustle of city life, setting out to find a suitable surface. Like an old-fashioned rag-and-bone collector tramping the city streets in search of discarded junk, it may purloin anything from a sand dollar (a burrowing sea urchin) to half a coconut shell, or even tin cans and pieces of plastic. It then pushes the object back to the anemone, although some objects are less easy for a fish to transport than others, much to the amusement of Roger Munns and producer Jonathan Smith.

'This was my favourite character in all the filming for "Reef",' says Jonathan. 'Roger had described the behaviour to me but, when we first went down, the male clownfish swam away from his anemone and started to push a coconut shell. It sat inside it, kicking its tail, and looked as if it was

CLOWNFISH COLLECT (below)
1 The clownfish family with their sea anemone home on soft sand.
2 The fish search for an object with a suitable surface to attach eggs, but some are just too big.
3 A half coconut is collected and somehow pushed towards home.
4 Eggs are deposited, fertilised and guarded.

1

2

driving a coconut car. I almost choked laughing through the mouthpiece of my rebreather.

'It was sometimes hard to focus on getting the shots we needed,' Roger remembers, 'because the poor male anemone fish was so comical as he tried to push the huge – at least huge to him – coconut shell. I admired his tenacity and perseverance, but he really made hard work of it!'

Eventually, the fish brings back his chosen object and places it against the base of the anemone, cleaning the surface carefully so the eggs will stick firmly. When the time comes, the female clownfish and one of her partners nip at the host's tentacles closest to the chosen nest site and the anemone retracts them, giving enough space for the female to deposit her eggs on the flat surface, with the male following close behind, fertilising them as they go. She then leaves to feed. He remains to guard the nest, helped by the anemone whose tentacles reform into a protective umbrella.

The clownfish is one of several species of fish that deposit their eggs on a moveable 'tablet'. There is even one that 'sand-blasts' its egg-laying site so that it is squeaky clean. The Galapagos ringtail damselfish takes mouthfuls of grit and spits them repeatedly at the chosen surface. Fish are turning out to be more creative than we ever imagined.

3

4

Mesmerising Cuttlefish

SHAPE CHANGER (above) The broadclub cuttlefish switches between a range of colours, textures and shapes, the changes taking place in just a few seconds.

THE HYPNOTIST (opposite) Having hypnotised its prey (in this case a crab), the cuttlefish grabs it with a club of suckers on the end of a pair of extendable tentacles that shoot out at high speed from the centre of its eight arms.

While related to the humble snail, the cephalopods – the octopuses, squid and cuttlefish – are surprisingly smart, and their secret weapon is in their skin. These characters have a whole range of skin cells that interact in different ways with light. The most obvious of these are chromatophores, pigment cells that can expand and contract in milliseconds so the animal's skin colour can change in an instant. Some patterns serve to camouflage the animal, a vanishing trick to suit any background, while others provide a means to communicate, signalling a warning or a courtship display. The changing patterns can also be used to bamboozle prey, and one species that uses this to a remarkable degree is the broadclub cuttlefish, found on coral reefs in the Indo-Pacific region from Mozambique right across to Fiji.

The cuttlefish has a soft body, making it vulnerable to the clacking claws of its armoured prey, such as crabs and shrimps, so to gain the upper hand it displays rapidly changing patterns and textures on its skin, switching their function from camouflaged defence to lurid attack. When hunting, it approaches a target with its body and arms forming an arc. At its centre is the pair of grasping tentacles coiled and ready to fire. It stalks its prey, switching on a mesmerising display of rapidly changing skin patterns. Black-and-white chevrons sweep across its head and down its arms like a neon light display at a fairground. The crustacean is thought to be hypnotised and becomes rooted to the spot. The cuttlefish shoots out its tentacles and immobilises its confused quarry. Dinner is served!

A Place of Giants

Not all the animals seen on a coral reef are permanent residents. Many others come and go, often attracted by seasonal gluts of food, and one of the most dramatic aggregations is that of manta rays in the Maldives.

In Hanifaru Bay, the corals form a funnel-shaped lagoon, about the size of a soccer field, where the incoming tide concentrates huge clouds of plankton. The first few mantas appear just after high tide, followed by bigger groups until there can be as many as 200 individuals feeding at the same time.

Most are reef mantas, but there are also a few oceanic mantas. Both are filter feeders. They plough through the plankton soup, the horn-like cephalic fins on either side of their heads funnelling the food into their letterbox-shaped mouths.

In a graceful underwater ballet, some rays swoop in and then loop-the-loop, scooping up plankton as they go. Others skim the seabed, swimming just millimetres above the sand, and a few target plankton swarms at the surface. Sometimes they feed together. When the plankton swarms thicken, many mantas form into long feeding chains, and when conditions are especially favourable, more than fifty rays spiral up in what is called 'cyclone feeding'. As they spin around in tight formation, they create a vortex, concentrating the food and sucking it in with their great, gaping mouths. When the feeding is good, a reef manta can consume 27 kilograms of plankton in a day, and if it is really good whale sharks also turn up and join in the feast. Big fish, big appetites! Hanifaru really is a place of giants.

VORTEX FEEDING (above) A group of manta rays feeds on plankton by swirling around in a circle and creating a whirlpool that concentrates the food.

LINE ASTERN (opposite) A flotilla of mantas swoops down in a long feeding chain.

A Night on the Reef

Like any big city, the reef never sleeps, although its inhabitants do – in shifts. At the first hint of darkness, the daytime crew takes cover and some of the sleepers are remarkably innovative. The parrotfish finds a safe crevice and surrounds itself with a sleeping bag of mucus that it exudes from its mouth. This cocoon serves two purposes: as an early warning system and as a containment vessel. If a moray eel comes calling and touches the mucus, the parrotfish is out of there pronto. The cocoon also prevents its body odour from drifting over the reef and attracting the attention of the night-hunting alley gangs and solitary killers – the sharks.

Lone tiger sharks come in from the open sea at high tide, orderly schools of grey reef sharks patrol the drop-off into deep water, frenetic mobs of blacktip reef sharks sweep the shallow, sandy reef flats, and in amongst the coral heads are gangs of whitetip reef sharks. The whitetips target squirrelfish and soldierfish, relatively small silver-orange fish with big eyes, which emerge at night to feed, but there is another night-time predator for which they really must watch out.

The bobbit is a horrific, metre-long iridescent worm. There are records from Japan of these rainbow-coloured monsters of the reef growing to 3 metres long and weighing 4 kilograms. It is said to get its unusual name from Mr J. W. and Mrs L. Bobbit, the former having cheated on the latter and the latter having cut off the penis of the former in revenge. It draws a parallel with the bobbit's formidable jaws.

The worm is an ambush predator, living in a mucus-lined burrow in the seabed; where it sits and waits, hidden by sand and gravel with only its five antennae showing. When its senses are triggered, the worm torpedoes out of its hole and, in a split second, turns its pharynx inside out, exposing a pair of scissor-like jaws and serrated, hook-shaped appendages. The attack is so fast and fierce a small fish can be sliced in half. Prey is dragged below the sand, preventing its escape, and just to make sure, the worm injects toxins, which kill or paralyse it.

Victims seem helpless when faced by such a ruthless and brutal predator, but there is at least one that fights back. Peters' monocle bream mobs the bobbit. If the fish finds a bobbit's lair, it hovers vertically, head down, and blows water into the hole, and soon several bream gather to join in the water fight. The bobbit's senses become overwhelmed, causing it to retract deep into its tunnel until the fish have gone.

Head-Bangers

The night is a risky time to be out and about and, like the no-go areas of a sprawling city, many parts of the reef are best avoided; yet nighttime is when many of its inhabitants choose to reproduce, and sometimes they do so in the most exposed of places. Triggered as often as not by the phases of the moon, daytime residents emerge from their nocturnal hiding places and put themselves at considerable risk in order to give their offspring the best start in life.

Since competition is so intense and legions of predators come in all shapes and sizes on the reef itself, ironically the best place for the next generation to develop and grow is in the relative safety of the open ocean. There are predators out there too, but they are far less concentrated. An added bonus is that sometimes ocean currents carry a larva to pastures new, so reef animals that take part in spawning events will do their best to ensure their fertilised eggs and larvae are carried away from the crowded reef.

Just before dawn, around the time of the full moon, at Sipadan, an oceanic island off the east coast of Sabah in Malaysian Borneo, groups of mature humphead parrotfish abandon their regular night-time hiding

BATTERING RAM (below) The male humphead or bumphead parrotfish has a hardened patch on its forehead that is used in a similar way to the horns of a mountain sheep.

HUMPHEADS (above) A group of male humphead parrotfish gathers at dawn on a shallow reef at Sipadan in the Celebes Sea.

places in caves and shipwrecks and begin to gather at the edge of the reef, where steep coral cliffs drop off into deep water. This is one of the most dangerous parts of the reef at night, the haunt of local grey reef sharks, yet the humpheads seem oblivious to the dangers for it is one of the best sites to scatter their spawn into the sea.

Male humpheads wear their good looks on their heads, and fight for the right to be top fish. The huge, bony bump on their forehead is the weapon of choice. It is used not only to break coral when feeding, but also to head-bang with the other males. Humpheads fight first and spawn later. They are living battering rams, and to establish who is the strongest and fittest they go in for head-butting contests like those of bighorn sheep, when males fight for the right to mate with the females. The humphead's bump even has a vertical bony ridge similar to the sheep's horns, and the male packs quite a punch. The blows can be so powerful the 'thwack' can be heard clearly underwater from some distance away. It is the only fish known to conduct this kind of aggressive head-butting behaviour using a specially adapted part of its body.

Nuptials reach a crescendo when a male and female fish leave the school and swim front-to-front up to within a metre of the surface, their eggs and sperm intermingling behind them. The fertilised eggs drift away in the current, soon hatching into tiny larvae that feed on phytoplankton at the ocean surface. Weeks later, they head inshore to mangrove forests and seagrass meadows, where they develop and grow, eventually returning to a coral reef to live out the rest of their lives.

Ambush at South Pass

At Fakarava Atoll in French Polynesia, spawning is an even more boisterous affair. Around the full moon in July, thousands of camouflage groupers head for South Pass, a narrow channel just 100 metres wide and 30 metres deep that connects the central lagoon to the open ocean. Twice each day, water rushes through the pass as the lagoon fills and drains with the tide, and it is here that male and female groupers congregate to spawn, the females noticeably bigger, with their bellies swollen with eggs.

After a few trial runs, when a few pairs leave the group in sudden bursts of speed to release their eggs and milt, this sparks the dramatic main event. At its peak on the outgoing tide, when thousands of fish spawn at roughly the same time, the water turns into a dense white fog. Fertilised

FEEDING FRENZY (below)
At Fakarava, grey reef sharks hunt spawning fish.

eggs are flushed out to sea by the strong current, but this mass-spawning event is what the local sharks have been waiting for.

Hundreds of grey reef sharks crowd into the pass, and they come because the groupers are so intent on spawning that they can be picked off with ease. They sweep in at high speed and grab the spawning fish before they have time to escape. Sharks flash past this way and that, as their targets rocket up towards the surface. Large blacktip and sicklefin lemon sharks swim in from the ocean and join the fray, and such is the mayhem even great hammerheads have been known to prey upon the sharks that are themselves hunting the groupers.

That there are so many sharks here is a bit of a biological puzzle. On average, 600 grey reef sharks are found here throughout the year, but numbers can vary between 250 in summer to as many as 700 of these 2-metre-long predators in winter. It is the highest concentration of grey reef sharks in the world, and there should not be enough food to maintain such numbers.

Scientists studying the sharks estimate that the population requires about 90 tonnes of food a year to stay healthy, but there is only about 17 tonnes available, so for most of the year the sharks must travel away from the channel and seek food elsewhere. However, for a couple of months in winter they don't. They stay put, and they can do so because of the groupers.

Like the delivery van arriving with the groceries, upwards of 17,000 camouflage groupers congregate in the channel. They come from all over Fakarava Atoll and nearby islands, some travelling from reefs as far as 50 kilometres away, and they represent a sudden influx of about 30 tonnes of available food. And even when the groupers have left, the sharks can turn their attention to the surgeonfish, parrotfish and several other species that also gather here to spawn. All these reef fish supplement the shark's normal diet, explaining why so many sharks are seen here.

Fakarava is unusual in that it has not been overfished. Just ten fishermen catch reef fish for subsistence, and the sharks are protected because French Polynesians revere them, so the grouper population has remained healthy. Significantly, on coral islands where overfishing has reduced populations of reef fish, including groupers, the shark population has also often suffered. The sharks at many of these places, of course, have been caught for their fins, decimating populations, but this research is showing that a ban on shark fishing alone might not be sufficient to protect them. The coral reef fishes that form these spawning aggregations must be protected too. Without them, there would not be so many sharks, and sharks are vital to the health of the coral reef community.

Trouble at the reef

The most fundamentally important animals on the reef are the polyps of hard, reef-building corals. Without them there would be no reef. They are actually tiny soft-bodied invertebrates that resemble miniature sea anemones, their evolutionary cousins, which at their base secrete a hard layer of calcium carbonate. It is this layer that forms the basic structure of the reef, and without these little chaps there would be nowhere for its myriad creatures to live.

Corals depend on sunlight and clear, warm seas. The polyps need sunlight because they are packed with single-celled, symbiotic dinoflagellates, called zooxanthellae, which live in their tissues. They manufacture food by photosynthesis, and the coral polyps obtain up to 90 per cent of their energy from them. The remaining nutrients come from food particles trapped by the polyp's tentacles. Without their tiny lodgers the polyps would be unable to grow fast enough to build and maintain the massive reef structures we see today, yet the polyp-zooxanthellae relationship is a fragile co-existence.

CATASTROPHE (below) Branching corals at Lizard Island on the Great Barrier Reef have bleached.

If polyps are stressed by change for sustained periods, such as significantly warmer or colder water, pollution, or smothering by sediment from rivers, they expel their zooxanthellae, a process known as 'bleaching'. The corals literally turn white, since the sunlight-harvesting pigments in the zooxanthellae give corals their colour. The corals are not necessarily dead and can survive short periods of elevated temperatures however, if temperatures remain high for extended periods of time they will bleach permanently and die. Corals often live just below levels that can cause thermal stress and are therefore highly vulnerable to climate change and coral bleaching.

Australia's Great Barrier Reef is currently reeling from the worst bleaching event in its history, according to the Great Barrier Reef Marine Park Authority. In the northern part of the reef, 95 per cent of corals have been damaged, including the home of Percy the tuskfish.

'What was heartbreaking was hearing, a couple of months after finishing filming on the Great Barrier Reef, that a whole section of reef had bleached, including Percy's castle.' RACHEL BUTLER, Assistant Producer

'What was heartbreaking,' reflects Rachel Butler, 'was hearing, a couple of months after finishing filming on the Great Barrier Reef, that a whole section of reef had bleached, including Percy's castle. It brought it home to us that our oceans – and coral reefs in particular – are so fragile and precious.'

For series researcher Yoland Bosiger it was especially distressing. 'I grew up in Port Douglas, so getting the call telling me that Lizard Island in the northern part of the Great Barrier Reef was experiencing the worst bleaching event in decades was quite simply horrifying, the worst day while working on this series. The thing is, we still know so little about these reefs. I had made more than 500 dives at Lizard Island, but it was not until we started to look for the unusual behaviours featured in *Blue Planet II* that I realised not only were coral groupers hunting with octopuses on a regular basis, but also there was a tuskfish using tools right on the very reef where I had conducted my research. It emphasised to me

PRE-BLEACHED CORAL (above) Filming unbleached corals was to become a rarity in some parts of the Great Barrier Reef, after back to back mass bleaching events.

WARMING OCEAN (above) Searching for corals that have not bleached at Port Douglas.

how little we know about coral reefs and how much there is still left to discover – that is, if the reefs survive.'

Even so, for all their fragility, corals are enormously resilient and can bounce back from, say, a single major change. Nowadays, though, they are being hit by more frequent changes in the environment – one day heatwaves and cyclones, the next day an outbreak of voracious crown-of-thorns starfish: it's death by a thousand cuts. And coral reefs, as we have learned, are the ocean's pharmacopoeia. If we lose them, the twenty-first century's medicine cabinet starts to look bare.

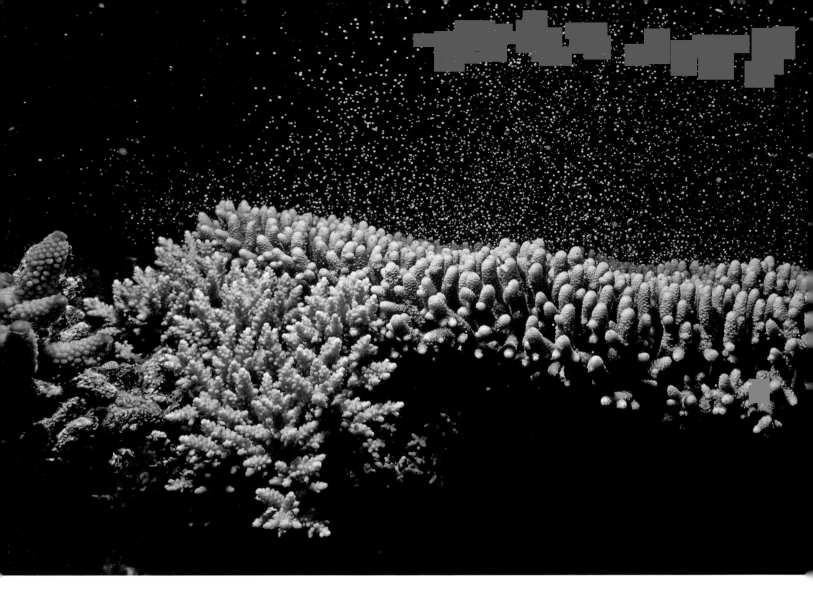

Upside Down Snowstorm

Coral bleaching has had less impact on the southern sector of Australia's Great Barrier Reef in 2016 compared with the north, and the corals here are able to complete their normal annual cycle. At night, just after a full moon, when the water temperature is rising, they gear up for one of the most spectacular displays by a marine creature.

Corals are flamboyant at the best of times, but during spawning they surpass themselves in the mother of all mass spawning events. Each polyp taking part in the show releases a tiny package of eggs or sperm into the water. It resembles a blizzard, except the snowfall is upwards and the snow is not only white but also red, yellow and orange. The little bundles float slowly towards the surface where fertilisation then takes place.

Yoland Bosiger has seen many of these mass-spawning events during her time as a dive-master and marine biologist on the Great Barrier Reef, and each time seems more impressive than the last. While filming for *Blue Planet II*, she and the crew witnessed a particularly spectacular event.

COLOURED BLIZZARD (above left)
Many corals of the Great Barrier Reef spawn at the same time, on the same night, guided by water temperature, the tides and the phases of the Moon.

CORAL HIGH SPOT (above right)
Corals synchronise the release sperm and eggs that float away in the water column.

'There was so much spawn in the water, that I could only make out the outline of the cameraman just a metre below me. It really was like being in a blinding snowstorm.'

An event like this can last several days, with particular species spawning on different days, a guard against hybridisation, and it can occur in different months depending on location. All the inshore reefs blast off around the first full moon in October. The outer reefs explode in November and December and, while the phases of the moon and temperature are the main stimuli, day length, salinity and the height of the tide can also influence whether an event will happen.

When an egg is fertilised it develops into a coral larva, known as a planula, which, like the fish larvae, is swept out into the open ocean where it drifts around on the ocean currents until it is ready to settle. When it does finally reach a reef, it must be ready to compete with already established residents. However, finding a suitable reef to call home presents the first challenge, and one cue that guides the larva is the noise of the dusk and dawn chorus.

Returning Home

Scientists have found that when the free-swimming larvae of corals, fish, crabs and lobsters return from the open ocean, they can use sounds from the reef to select and locate a suitable place to settle.

Larvae probably detect the sounds made by adult fish and many of the reef's invertebrate species, including snapping shrimp and gnawing sea urchins, which provide a beacon to guide their return. The sounds may even be imprinted on them. Clownfish embryos respond to sounds for a whole week, so before they get washed out into the open ocean they might develop a 'memory' of their home reef, the place where their parents lived and had successfully reproduced. When close to a reef with a similar soundscape, it's an indication that it's the right place to go to. The reef sounds also induce a change in swimming behaviour, and cause the larvae to change anatomically and physiologically into a form ready to settle on the reef.

As soon as they reach the reef, some fish begin to make sounds themselves. Like youngsters the world over, fish larvae are exceptionally noisy. Young grey snappers, for example, produce 'knock' and 'growl' sounds that are similar to those of their parents. The chorus occurs at night, so it is thought to be a way in which snapper larvae stay together, seeking protection in a group while so young and vulnerable.

The downside of this reliance on auditory cues is that the sounds made by humans, such as the noise from ships' engines, motorboats, pile drivers and wind turbines, could interfere with the ability of larvae to find the right reef on which to settle. The upside is that, by broadcasting the relevant sounds underwater, scientists learn to play Pied Piper, attracting larvae to reefs that have been damaged by bleaching, like those in the northern part of the Great Barrier Reef, to help them recover.

Either way, what is exciting scientifically is the prospect of a tiny fish larva hearing the sound of its own species, rather than those of predators, or hearing the general sound of the reef to assess its quality, and that this might incline it to settle in a particular spot. It was once thought that the way larvae landed on a reef was pure luck. Evidently it's not... These tiny fish have far greater control over their destiny.

NEW LIFE (right) Clownfish larvae develop inside their transparent eggs, prior to their sojourn in the open ocean and eventual return to a coral reef.

chapter four
Green Seas

KELP ISLANDS (left) Juvenile fish from the kelp forest follow a 'kelp paddy', which has ripped away from the near-shore kelp forest and drifted out to sea.

KELP FOREST (previous page) Off the coast of California, close to San Francisco, young fish hide amongst fronds of giant kelp.

t is often said that tropical rainforests are the 'lungs' of the Earth, but this is only part of the story. The oceans play an even greater role in regulating the levels of oxygen and the greenhouse gas carbon dioxide in the atmosphere. Marine life, including the tiniest plant-like organisms in the phytoplankton, produce almost half the oxygen on the planet and absorbs a third of the carbon dioxide emitted since the Industrial Revolution. Up to 70 per cent of that carbon dioxide is captured and stored by seagrass meadows, salt marshes and mangroves or recycled by kelp forests, yet these 'blue forests', as they are known, cover less than 0.5 per cent of the Earth's surface. They may be small but they are vital to the health of our planet, and they are under threat. Rising sea levels and widespread coastal development, to name just two pressures, are squeezing out Earth's other lung. UNESCO has warned that this will magnify existing environmental stresses, jeopardise food security, trigger conflict over resources, and contribute to the loss of livelihood for countless millions of people. This is how vital the health of every kelp forest, mangrove swamp, seagrass meadow and bloom of phytoplankton is to us and to the rest of life on our planet.

Too Much of a Good Thing

High productivity along this coast, particularly off Namibia, can sometimes have its downside. In addition to upwellings, rivers are another source of nutrients, but there can be too much of a good thing. Rivers can bring death. Agricultural run-off can feed too much fertiliser into the sea, enabling phytoplankton to bloom big time, a veritable feast for the zooplankton and the fish that feed on them. But what if there is more food than the fish can eat or if populations of these plankton-eating fish have been drastically reduced by overfishing? It leads eventually to a heavy fall of dead plankton, and the bacteria involved in their decay use up all the oxygen. Anaerobic bacteria take over and they produce hydrogen sulphide, which builds on the ocean floor until it erupts, killing any fish that survived the overfishing and the low oxygen conditions, a treble whammy.

Local fishermen know when these mass die-offs are about to occur for the 'bad eggs' aroma of hydrogen sulphide pervades their villages. NASA can spot them from satellites in Earth orbit. Whichever way they are observed, they mean entire villages might go hungry, and the kelp forest loses its resident and visiting fish, affecting the entire ecosystem.

CHOKED SEA (below) Seen from space, fertilisers in agricultural run-off and sewage from the town have caused a vigorous bloom of algae and bacteria on this stretch of coast. Oxygen is used up, effectively killing off most other marine life.

Where Giants Grow

PACIFIC MONSTER (above) A giant Pacific octopus goes hunting. Aside from the regular fare of crabs and lobsters, it can catch small sharks, such as spiny dogfish, and has even been seen to capture a seagull.

Kelp is fussy about where it lives. Conditions have to be just right. It is found generally in shallow, clear temperate and polar seas, rarely deeper than 40 metres, in places where upwellings flood the forest with nutrients, and, crucially, the water temperature is less than 20°C. These key conditions are met on the Pacific coast of North America, where there are possibly the most extensive tracts of kelp forest in the world. They stretch from Alaska in the north to Baja California in the south, and they are formed from the largest species of kelp on Earth.

In higher latitudes in the northern part of the range, the dominant species is bull kelp, which grows up to 35 metres long. It is an annual, destroyed during winter storms, but in the autumn it drops a patch of spores right beside its dying remains, so the new kelp attaches to the right substrate and grows in exactly the right place in spring. As in many kelp forests, cephalopods are common, and the biggest species here is the giant Pacific octopus.

'When we got our eye in, we'd find a stationary octopus, disguised on the reef, and you could see the distinctive shapes of crabs and suchlike under the webbing between its arms, which it had still to consume.' JOHN CHAMBERS, Assistant Producer

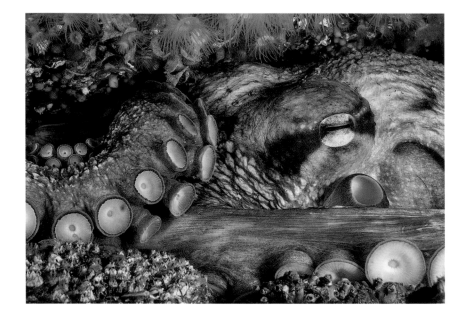

GIANT SEAWEED (opposite) Off the coast of British Columbia, the fronds of bull kelp form a forest canopy under which schooling black rockfish hang out.

GIANT'S LAIR (left) The giant Pacific octopus has a regular hiding place in the rocky reefs of the kelp forest.

With an arm span of up to 9.8 metres and weighing 136 kilograms, the giant Pacific octopus vies with the deep-sea seven-arm octopus for the title 'world's largest octopus', and it really made an impression on assistant producer John Chambers.

'The giant Pacific octopus doesn't seem to fit into any of the rules of other animals. It can change shape, colour, and texture and squeeze through anything that isn't bigger than its eye or beak. We would watch it creep across the rock wall, perfectly disguised and stalking prey ever so slowly. When it got close enough, it pounced at incredible speed, 'tenting' over its victim while its body flashed bright white, almost as if it was enraged.

'Most of the time, we failed to see the prey. We assumed it was hidden under the rocks. Other times, when we got our eye in, we'd find a stationary octopus, disguised on the reef, and you could see the distinctive shapes of crabs and suchlike under the webbing between its arms, which it had still to consume.

'There was one occasion, when we were still novices at finding the octopuses, when we arrived at a den site to see an octopus violently shaken by a California sea lion. We thought, "Great, there goes our star," but when we went underwater we discovered that the octopus we had been staking out was still there. The sea lions were clearly much better at finding them than we were!'

Kelp Forest Critters

In the southern sector of the Pacific coast, an even bigger species of kelp takes over. This is the giant kelp, a perennial that grows up to a staggering 50 centimetres per day, reaches a total length of 60 metres, and can live for up to ten years. It is one of the fastest-growing living things on the planet and the world's largest kelp.

Giant kelp, like other kelp species, looks superficially like a tree. It is anchored by holdfasts, which are not roots but finger-like projections that grasp the rocks on the seabed, and it grows towards the surface with a trunk-like stipe kept afloat with bladder buoyancy aids. At the top are branching blade-shaped fronds, like the leaves of a tree, and the analogy does not end there.

The kelp forest has similar levels as a tropical rainforest – canopy, understorey and forest floor. If the water is shallower than the seaweeds are long, their golden brown fronds spread across the sea's surface, forming a dense 'canopy' that is bathed in sunshine, but which blocks out the light to the layers below. Smaller kelp species occupy the understorey, while the relatively dark sea floor has low-growing red and green seaweeds, and, as in the rainforest, different groups of animals live at the different levels.

Amphipods known as 'skeleton shrimps' are so delicate and wispy that they almost disappear amongst the fronds, where mysids, kelp crabs and turban snails also live. The understorey plays host to many fish, such as the rockfish and sheepheads, while sea urchins and sea stars occupy the seabed, with kelp holdfasts sheltering more than 150 species of small invertebrates alone. They are such desirable places to hide, one survey revealed the holdfasts of just five giant kelps in Tasmania were playing host to 23,000 individuals.

Many of these critters live permanently amongst the kelp, while others visit to feed, spawn or provide their offspring with a safe place to grow, making it one of the most seasonally productive and diverse habitats in the ocean. It's thought that while the South African kelp forests have high productivity, these northeast Pacific forests have greater biodiversity. An unusual nudibranch lives here, for example, which has a very different feeding system from other sea slugs: instead of a rasping tongue for scraping algae from rocks, it has an oral hood.

SEE-THROUGH SEA SLUG (opposite) A 'bouquet' of translucent hooded nudibranchs on giant kelp sweeps the water with expanded oral hoods fringed with sensory tentacles. Each sea slug nets passing amphipods, copepods, mysids and other small crustaceans.

KELP GARDENS (below) The kelp forest floor is often a colourful mix of sea creatures, such as white plumose and red dahlia sea anemones.

The hooded nudibranch attaches itself firmly to a kelp frond and feeds on small crustaceans, such as copepods, by expanding its oral hood and sweeping it downwards like a net. As soon as something edible is trapped, the hood closes and its fringing tentacles force the prey into the animal's mouth. Fish, including kelp surfperch, kelp bass and giant kelpfish, patrol the canopy and they might well try to snatch the nudibranch, but it confuses an attacker by shedding the horn-like cerata on its back. These produce a sticky secretion at their tip and they wriggle for some time, distracting and maybe even repelling the fish, which enables the hooded nudibranch to slither away and live another day. On occasions, however, the nudibranch can get its own back. When tiny kelp bass larvae come into the forest, the hooded nudibranch is ready to snag them.

KELP CLIMBING CRABS (above) Several species of spider crabs live amongst the kelp, clambering slowly but deftly on the fronds and stapes. Some actually eat the kelp.

Night in the Forest

ELECTRIC SHOCKER (below) The Pacific electric ray swims amongst giant kelp off the coast of California. It propels itself along with its tail, and, it is neutrally buoyant, so it can hover in midwater with little effort.

At night, an especially spine-chilling member of the ray family is on the prowl – the Pacific torpedo or electric ray. Blocks of its muscles have switched from propelling it to charging it, its pair of kidney-shaped modified muscle batteries generating direct current pulses of 45 volts to knock out prey or to defend itself from attackers.

By day it hides on the forest floor and ambushes anything that swims within range. Its lateral line picks up movements in the water and the electroreceptors in its snout tell it whether the target is living. If so, it shoots forward, enveloping its victim with the disc of its body and then zaps it with electrical pulses that are strong enough to stun a human diver.

During the night it becomes an active hunter. It rises off the bottom, ready to intercept fish that are hiding in the understorey. It stalks a shoal, swimming slowly or drifting in the current, and when it is just 5 centimetres from the target it lunges forward, envelops the prey and stuns it with electric shocks. In order to swallow it head first, the ray flaps its tail causing the fish to flip over. It then turns unhurriedly to gulp down its meal.

Garibaldi Gardens

On the forest floor resides a fish with serious attitude. The bright orange Garibaldi is ready to fight all comers, and it all starts when the male Garibaldi reaches adulthood. He finds a suitable patch of reef, preferably sheltered against the storms. In March each year he tidies what will become his nest area, nibbling away most seaweeds, the exceptions being a few species of algae to which he takes a fancy. These are trimmed neatly, so they are a couple of centimetres long, and then the male is ready to attract a partner to his garden.

In early April, the females appear and, if they are suitably impressed with the male's gardening skills, they signal their interest by meandering nonchalantly nearby with their fins pointing straight up. The male responds by swimming in loops and making a thumping sound. If a female looks responsive, he swims to his garden, hoping she will follow, but females are very choosy and will visit up to fifteen gardens before they select one, and they are influenced not by the male's performance or the beauty of his garden, but by whether another female has already laid eggs there.

DAYGLO DAMSELS (below) The bright orange Garibaldi is the largest member of the damselfish family. It is the state fish of California, and is protected in Californian waters.

ON GUARD (above) Male garibaldis vigorously defend their nest sites, and will take on creatures much bigger than themselves, even human divers.

Females are reluctant to lay in an empty nest, so the male's first attempts to woo a female can be frustrating, but, should he become popular, the females will line up to deposit their eggs in his nest. In order to reach that stage, he must have freshly laid, bright yellow eggs in his nest, and then up to 20 females might lay in this single nest. He is fiercely territorial and will chase away the female the second she has finished laying. The BBC's film crew was equally unwelcome.

'The fish attacked the camera lenses,' recalls assistant producer Sarah Conner, 'and he even had a go at our facemasks. Maybe he saw his own reflection there. He was quite a character!'

But this meticulousness in protecting his offspring is the most important thing to him. He fertilises the eggs, and guards them carefully until they hatch out two to three weeks later. His territory appears to be well marked, for male Garibaldis living just 60 centimetres apart will graze peacefully on seaweeds, sponges, bryozoans and tubeworms and nibble at the tube feet of sea stars and sea urchins without coming to blows with their neighbours, but each must be careful to stick to his own patch. Up to forty can have territories in an area the size of a basketball court, splashes of glowing orange in a forest of browns and greens.

Urchins and Otters

SPIKY SCATTER CUSHIONS
(opposite) Sea urchins sometimes
proliferate in huge numbers.
Normally they are kept in check
by lobsters, sheephead fish and
sea otters.

TOOL-USER (below) A sea
otter floats on its back while
consuming a meal of sea urchin.

One of the common intruders on the male Garibaldi's territory is the sea urchin. One or two are easy to deal with. The fish picks them up in its mouth and carts them off. They are part of the local community, but there are times when the forest is overrun with them, particularly purple sea urchins, and this can be serious for the kelp and all the other creatures living in the kelp forest.

Sea urchins often eat the kelp holdfasts, and occasionally populations increase to such an extent that they destroy all these anchors. Great swathes of kelp forest are set free and washed away or thrown up on the shore. The reason for the population explosion is often due to a reduction in their primary predators, especially sea otters, enabling the sea urchins to proliferate unchecked.

Sea otters are a keystone species, one of the guardians of the kelp forest. To survive they must consume about 25 per cent of their bodyweight a day – the equivalent of a healthy 7-year-old child eating 80 quarter-pound hamburgers, and they do this by eating enormous numbers of sea urchins, as well as crabs, clams, mussels, abalone, shrimps and even fish. The hard-bodied items are smashed against a rock 'anvil' resting on the otter's stomach, making it one of the few marine mammals to use tools.

Sea otters tend to feed alone, but often rest together in single-sex groups known as 'rafts'. To prevent it from drifting out to sea, each otter wraps itself

in kelp fronds, so it is firmly anchored to the seabed. Male rafts tend to have more otters than female rafts, with large 'super-rafts' of young male otters sometimes numbering up to 2,000 animals, the largest raft ever known.

Numbers like these, however, have been rare over the past hundred years, for sea otters have had a really tough time. The problem is their coat. They're the 'teddy bears' of the ocean. Unlike other marine mammals, they do not have a layer of blubber under the skin; instead, they have extremely thick fur. A couple of square centimetres can have more than a million hairs, about ten times as many as you have on your head, and this was their downfall. From the eighteenth to the early twentieth century, sea otters were killed for their fur, and at one point fewer than 2,000 individuals survived. Conservation efforts brought them back from the brink, and, during the twentieth century, numbers rebounded to two-thirds of their former range, a conservation success story.

Nevertheless, the International Union for the Conservation of Nature (IUCN) still classifies them as 'endangered'. They are especially vulnerable to poaching, oil spills and entanglement in fishing gear. In southern California toxoplasmosis and parasitic worms are a problem, while in the northern part of their range, a new factor has had a significant impact on populations.

Off the coast of southeast Alaska, killer whales now hunt sea otters. It's a surprising development. Sea otters probably do not taste good and they are barely a mouthful for an animal as large as a killer whale, but the blubber-

OTTER RAFTS (below) Sea otters prevent themselves from drifting out to sea by using fronds of giant kelp as anchor lines.

rich seals and sea lions on which these black-and-white killers normally feed are also in short supply. In turn, the seals and sea lions have declined, probably because of overfishing in the North Pacific. Their normal prey, such as pollack, has been fished down. It is a chain of events that shows how animals in different parts of the ocean, both in offshore and nearshore waters, are dependent on each other.

The upshot of all this is that sea otter numbers are taking a second tumble, and in parts of the kelp forest where they are missing, the sea urchins take over. The underwater seascape becomes what scientists call 'urchin barrens', just carpets of sea urchins and very little else, and they will stay that way until the current crop of adult urchins has died out. The barren landscape is not suitable for sea urchin larvae to settle, so the kelp has a chance to bounce back before the next invasion. It has led some scientists to wonder whether this is part of a natural cycle of good times and bad.

Winter Storms

A key facet of the natural cycle in these kelp forests is the winter storm. During the last quarter of the year, things liven up considerably on North America's Pacific coast. Autumn and winter storms, known locally as 'Big Blows', often start in October and are most prevalent in December. These windstorms whip up the waves and pulverise kelp forests, ripping holdfasts away from the rocks and shredding fronds. Much is dumped on nearby beaches, to become the domain of kelp flies and sand hoppers, but large

TORN KELP (above) Powerful storms tear the kelp from the seabed and dump some of it on nearby beaches.

KELP PADDY (overleaf) Floating islands of drifting kelp are hosts to temporary ecosystems containing many types of marine creatures, especially juvenile fish.

rafts of floating kelp, known as 'kelp paddies', drift out into the ocean forming their own temporary, self-contained ecosystems. Small inshore fish and invertebrates trapped in the kelp drift with them, and the floating paddy attracts the ocean's pelagic predators, such as tuna and marlin. They drift southwards until they reach warmer waters and most of them rot and break up, but if some of the kelp survived and continued to float on the ocean currents could this be the way giant kelp established itself in other parts of the world?

lemon-shaped white eggs. Each egg is treated separately. The female takes an egg, passes it over her sperm receptacle, and then attaches it to the underside of rocks in caves and crevices. It's a bittersweet affair: the cuttlefish fast during the breeding season, and their condition deteriorates to such an extent that they die shortly afterwards.

At one time, hundreds of thousands of cuttlefish joined the gathering, but in recent years considerably fewer have returned to breed each season, thanks, it is thought, partly to overfishing, although water temperature and salinity could

WINTER MATING (below) A group of giant cuttlefish appears to rest during a pause in the frantic courtship activity that occurs on this rocky reef in winter.

also be factors. Nobody is sure. Like the South African octopuses, however, the cuttlefish are caught wholesale and used as bait for catching snappers, a fish with which they seem to have an ecological link. As snapper numbers rise and fall, so do cuttlefish numbers. Cuttlefish populations have been recovering in recent years, which appears to coincide with the banning of fisheries, but they are not yet at the numbers they once were. It is another threat to kelp forests and their inhabitants.

ANIMATED SEAWEED (below) A relative of the seahorse, the weedy sea dragon has leaf-like flaps that are not used for swimming; instead, they help camouflage the fish amongst the kelp or seagrass in which it lives.

Marine Meadows

A second major 'blue forest' is the seagrass meadow. These are found in sheltered, shallow waters from the Arctic to the tropics, and form huge meadows that can be seen from space. Antarctica is the only continent not to have them.

Seagrass looks like seaweed, but it is a grass-like flowering plant with stems, leaves, flowers and seeds. There are many species and they are the main plants in an ecosystem that has received little attention in the past, yet harbours an incredibly diverse community of marine life and is a major nursery area for baby fish, including commercially important species. It has been estimated that a single hectare of healthy seagrass meadow can be

'I have to admit, the weedy sea dragon didn't do a whole lot, and the hardest thing was to find them, as they are so well camouflaged and they drift about in the current like seaweed, sometimes buffeted by the surge.' JOHN CHAMBERS, Assistant Producer

home to around 80,000 small fish and over 100 million tiny invertebrates. In South Australia, it is a hiding place for the weedy sea dragon.

Unlike the closely related seahorses, which have a prehensile tail able to grasp seaweeds, the weedy sea dragon drifts in the current. Its body is festooned with leafy appendages so the fish resembles floating and swaying seaweed, and it feeds by sucking zooplankton and tiny crustaceans into its toothless mouth, as John Chambers could clearly see when the high-speed cameras revealed the detail.

'I have to admit, the weedy sea dragon didn't do a whole lot, and the hardest thing was to find them, as they are so well camouflaged and they drift about in the current like seaweed, sometimes buffeted by the surge.

'When they were feeding, they were like hummingbirds, floating in the water column and pecking at mysid shrimps. They strike unbelievably quickly; we had to film at high speed, just to see what was going on. They have extraordinarily hydrodynamic snouts, which suck in their prey at an incredible speed. After seeing them gently gliding along, it was interesting to see them strike so quickly.'

HARD TO FIND (above) The film crew discovers this sea dragon in a scrappy seagrass meadow off South Australia.

The male sea dragon looks after the fertilised eggs, not in a pouch like seahorses, but tucked under his tail, and it sometimes comes across something unusual: its eggs become covered in algae. Whether this is the product of a warmer sea or increased light levels in shallow water, nobody knows, but it could be a potential hazard.

'The time that the algae caused a problem,' John could see, 'was when the sea dragons were hatching. The tiny babies struggled to get away. Their tails became stuck in the algae as they tried to break free.'

The algae also cover the seagrass and, although it's an inconvenience for the young sea dragons, it is food for young fish and invertebrates living in the meadow. In fact, scientists now think that some of the larger animals feeding on the seagrass, such as green sea turtles and dugongs, actually obtain much of their nutrients, not from the seagrass leaves themselves, but from the 'micro-forest' of epiphytic algae.

PLOUGHING THE SEABED (below)
The dugong uses its upper lip to tear away the seagrass, and leaves behind a distinct furrow or 'feeding trail' on the sea floor.

Seed-Spreading Turtles

Green sea turtles are carnivorous for the first part of their lives. As juveniles they feed on sponges, jellyfish, fish eggs, molluscs, worms, and crustaceans, but when they reach adulthood, they switch to a predominantly herbivorous diet, chomping on seagrass and algae, and that's not all. Aside from regularly trimming the seagrass meadow, they appear to have an important role in spreading it. It was once thought that only ocean currents dispersed seagrass seeds, but evidence is accumulating that turtles, and some of the other seagrass consumers, are at least partly responsible. The average green turtle eats about 2 kilograms of leaves and defecates about 25 seeds

UNDERWATER MOWER (above) An adult green sea turtle chomps on seagrass. It bites off the tips of the blades of grass with its serrated jaw, which, like a well-mown lawn, keeps the meadow healthy.

a day, and turtles tend to return to areas where seagrass traditionally grows, so they reseed old grounds as well as starting new ones.

Furthermore, in the laboratory, seeds germinate faster after having passed through the turtle's gut. Seagrasses evolved about 100 million years ago and turtles have been eating seagrass for close to 50 million years, so it is possible the two species have co-evolved.

There is always the danger, of course, that an overly large population of turtles would strip out all of the seagrass, whether they replant it or not, but nature has an answer for that too. Tiger sharks protect the seedlings by keeping turtles in check!

Saw-Teeth

Tiger sharks have the dental wherewithal to slice into a turtle shell. Their teeth are shaped like those in a chainsaw, so they would also make short work of a dugong. In aptly named Shark Bay, on the coast of Western Australia, dugongs, turtles and tiger sharks perform a deadly ballet. The sharks patrol the lush parts of the seagrass meadows because that is where they expect the turtles and dugongs to be feeding, but the prey is smarter than that. If tiger sharks are in the vicinity, healthy turtles and dugongs tend to crop the poorer quality seagrass in deeper water at the edge of the meadow. Here they have a chance to outmanoeuvre the sharks. Animals in poor condition, however, risk an attack by foraging in the high-quality centre of the meadow.

The sharks also ensure that turtles keep moving around, which means they may inadvertently help to disperse the seagrass seeds far and wide, and the turtles do not overgraze any one part of the meadow. Tiger sharks are often painted as the villains, but they not only help to keep seagrass meadows in good shape, but also weed out the old and infirm to maintain the health of local populations of green sea turtles and dugongs.

In Bermuda and in parts of the Indian Ocean, where shark populations have dropped due to overfishing, entire seagrass meadows have disappeared. This is how important the tiger sharks are, but their absence is not the only cause. Rising sea levels and the destruction of coastal habitats by new building developments, such as tourist resorts, flood defences and aquaculture ponds, are having an impact. Dredging and other human activities, including recreational boats operating in waters that are too shallow, destroy an area of seagrass the size of two soccer pitches every hour of the day, and this is serious.

Seagrass meadows, more so than kelp forests, contribute to the balance of gases in the atmosphere. Through the process of photosynthesis, just a square metre generates 10 litres of oxygen every day, all the while trapping carbon dioxide, and although seagrass meadows cover just 0.1 per cent of the seabed, they are responsible for 11–12 per cent of the organic carbon locked up in the ocean. It has been estimated that all these seagrass meadows capture 27.4 million tonnes of carbon each year. It is one of the world's most important carbon sinks, and without them our atmosphere would be transformed, and not for the good, yet, in the recent past, we have paid little heed to them.

SEA TIGER (left) At over 5 metres long, the tiger shark is a formidable predator. It is one of the few sharks that can slice into turtle shells.

Saltwater Trees

It is not only grass that grows in the sea; there are also trees, and they capture carbon too, the third 'blue forest'. Coastal habitats like mangroves absorb and store fifty times more carbon than the same area of tropical rainforest, making them another vital part of the ocean-atmosphere system.

Mangroves are odd trees, however. They can tolerate salt but not frost, preferring water temperatures above 20°C in winter in places free of strong wave action and currents, so you find them in tropical and subtropical shallow coastal or brackish intertidal zones. They grow successfully in saltwater, for they can lose salt from glands in their leaves or deposit it in their bark, stems, or roots, or in dying leaves that later fall off the tree. They can also withstand extreme changes in salinity, air temperature and moisture during the rise and fall of the tides, but not all species are the same.

Mangroves have a salt filtration and root system that varies between species. Red mangroves, for example, have stilt-like roots that can absorb air through pores in their bark. They thrive in the most inundated areas. Black mangroves occur on higher ground and have pneumatophores or breathing

FIRST DEFENCE (below) Mangroves form a buffer zone between land and sea. They absorb the energy from storms and waves, protecting the coastline.

BABY FISH NURSERY (above)
The tangle of mangrove roots is a good hiding place for young fish, and it traps nutrient-rich sediments to the benefit of the entire ecosystem.

tubes that stick up out of the ground. Both are important in stabilising coastlines, for they can be in place for many years, and they nurture a relatively stable ecosystem, the dead leaves and other detritus building a nutrient-rich mud on the seabed.

Mangrove roots trap sediments and are a protective buffer between the turbulent ocean and the fragile shore, and, like kelp and seagrass, the tangle of mangrove roots is home to a large and varied marine community, including mangrove crabs, mudskippers, and a host of baby fish. A large number of tropical fish spend their formative years in amongst the mangroves. The fish, however, are compromised at low tide, for the mangrove roots and mud are exposed to the air. Deprived temporarily of their safe haven, they must venture out across the mud or sand and right into the firing line of waiting predators.

chapter five
Big Blue

LETTERBOX MOUTH (left) The head of the world's largest living fish, the whale shark, along with its entourage of pilot fish.

WHALE OF A TAIL (previous page) The enormous tail of a sperm whale propels it through the water at a cruising speed of about 10 mph.

F ar from the land is the 'great blue', where hurricane-force winds can whip up 30-metre-high rogue waves and produce chasm-like troughs that have engulfed great ships, lost without trace. The biggest test for wildlife out here is not tumultuous storms, though, but the apparent emptiness. The challenge is how to survive in what at first sight seems an endless blue desert, but in reality is not.

Featureless though the open ocean might seem to us, it is not to marine life. It has a structure. Animals know their way around in the same way that we find our way about in a familiar country – they have mental maps, and there is food here... somewhere. The ocean's animals know where to look for it, find it and catch it, yet try to stay off the menu themselves. It is the realm not only of the superfast and the supercharged, like slender fin whales and swordfish, but also of the laidback 'drifters', like jellyfish and salps, and of strategic extremes in the battle to stay alive in a place where their next meal may be weeks in coming – or may even be them!

A Whale Called Digit

It is siesta time in the ocean off the Caribbean island of Dominica. A baby sperm whale sleeps vertically in the water, her head pointing upwards. She was nicknamed Digit by scientists from the Dominica Sperm Whale Project (DSWP) based at Denmark's Aarhus University. Nearby, her mother, known as Fingers, and several other whales from 'the 'Group of Seven', probably the best studied sperm whales in the world, are sleeping too, some with the tips of their noses poking above the surface, others with their tail uppermost. Who knows of what they dream or if they even do, although they do experience REM sleep, which is associated with dreaming in people; but whatever they do, they do it with the largest brain in the world, five times bigger than a human's, for these are big animals.

The sperm whale is the world's largest living toothed hunter, with mature males growing up to 18 metres long, females about a third smaller. Like most groups, this one has mainly adult females with a single calf, and for the moment they are out for the count. During sleep, they neither breathe nor move, but it is thought they do not doze for long: little over an hour a day in 10- to 15-minute naps, making them one of the least sleep-dependent mammals known.

The calf stirs. One eye opens, then the other. The adults gather around, socialising. The little one is the centre of their world, one of a family unit that seems to be more complex and interwoven even than our own. Family units in the Caribbean are made of a single female lineage: grandmothers, mothers and their immature offspring, and they all care for the calf, whether it is their baby or not; it's a bit like an entire village raising a single child.

Sperm whales, like us, also talk a lot. They have a language of click patterns, much like Morse code, and scientists believe that different patterns of sperm whale clicks, known as 'codas', have different meanings. In the eastern Caribbean, the whales have at least 22 different codas, but all of the whales use one particular coda with the pattern 'click-pause-click-pause-click-click-click'. This pattern has only been heard in the Caribbean, and is possibly a marker for that community of whales.

'Our recent research,' says Shane Gero, founder and principal investigator at DSWP, 'has shown that one coda might be used for individual

OCEAN GIANT (above) Female sperm whales are 11 metres long, and males measure 16 metres on average. They are the largest of the toothed whales.

recognition, like a first name, and another might function in family identity, like a surname. And we've found that calves, like Digit, take at least two years before they make the correct click patterns that sound like their mothers'. They babble at first before getting it right.'

Once Digit has mastered her clicks, she will able to communicate with other families that share the same coda types. They have the same 'dialect' and several of these families make up a 'clan'. Whales in different clans do things in their own way, and it shows not only in their dialects: their cultures are different. They differ in how they dive, what kind of squid they eat, their movement patterns, and how they socialise. When whale families gather together, they meet up with other families from their own clan but will avoid families from different clans. In other words, they remember their friends and relatives, even if they have been separated for many months or even years.

Shane and his colleagues have learned a lot about how whale families work by following their lives across decades spent at sea, but there are still many questions. An intriguing one is whether there are sperm whale matriarchs, as in elephant herds. With such a large brain, it is conceivable that the eldest female remembers places in the ocean where the best food is to be had, in the same way that the elephant matriarch remembers the best waterholes in times of drought. There is likely a great deal of traditional knowledge shared from one generation to the next, and this cultural wisdom is key to their survival.

When it comes to feeding time, sperm whales really do go to extremes. They head for the abyss, where sufficient quantities of food, in the shape of deep-sea squid and fish, can satisfy their gigantic appetites. It is one of nature's greatest feats of endurance, for the whales often dive as deep as a kilometre below the surface, and hold their breath for about 40 minutes while chasing and catching squid. It is such an alien world for humans; what happens down there has, until now, been speculation. However, by listening to their clicks, the scientists at DSWP are beginning to work things out, helped in part by the BBC's onboard underwater cameras.

A camera was attached to Fingers via four small suction cups. At first, the pictures show Fingers and Digit diving together. As if to reinforce the bond between them, the calf gently bumps and strokes her mother, the two chattering away in click codas, but the baby does not go all the way. She peels off and returns to the surface, where she awaits her mother's return.

Such is the importance of hunting in the deep, the family continues on together, leaving the calf exposed to the ocean's predators, but if the calf should cry out in distress, all the adult whales would be at her side in as many minutes as it takes to power up from the depths. But for now her mother continues down to 600–800 metres. This is where she starts to hunt.

Her communication calls stop and the clicks change to a slow metronome-like pattern of powerful clicks at a deafening 230 decibels in water. These are echolocation clicks. She probes the darkness, up to 120 metres ahead, or possibly even further, listening intently for the echoes. Rapid bursts of clicks indicate she has found a target and, as she closes in, she gathers more detailed information about its size, direction of travel and edibility. Then, there's silence. She's caught it!

CONSERVATION (above) A camera is attached to a sperm whale using suckers.

GETTING TOGETHER (opposite and overleaf) Sperm whales are very social animals. They are constantly touching, and even 'groom' each other, like apes do. They rub their bodies together to get rid of flaking skin.

Filming these enormous animals alongside Shane and his colleagues has been *Blue Planet II* producer John Ruthven and his crew. On one occasion, they were filming a family group of sperm whales and witnessed how the whales rub against each other, showing similar behaviour to apes grooming close relatives.

'Sperm whales are covered in flaking sheets of skin, something that's thought to prevent barnacles and parasites attaching and hindering swimming – a natural antifouling mechanism. Like all flaky skin, it probably gets itchy, and rubbing relieves the itch. Underwater we filmed large sheets of skin floating by. They looked like jellyfish lit by the sun. Behaviour like this reminds us, perhaps, of how intelligent sperm whales are, and how we might consider them in the same league as the great apes, even though they live in the ocean.'

The Greatest Migration on Earth

In the tropics and in temperate seas in summer, the uppermost layer of the open ocean is like a warm water 'skin', known popularly as the 'sunlight zone'. It sits on top of the cooler waters of the deep sea, the two separated by a boundary layer, called the thermocline.

When feeding, sperm whales have turned their backs on this sunlight zone, but other forms of marine life embrace it, for this is where the phytoplankton live. Dense blooms occur closer to the coast and near islands, where nutrients are stirred up from the deep, and at higher latitudes in summer, because of the long days and short nights. Distribution in the open ocean is patchy, with plankton concentrated at the boundaries between currents, akin to weather fronts in the atmosphere. Nevertheless, there is sufficient to trigger an extraordinary movement of animals.

Every day – in the morning and again in the evening – animals are on the move vertically. It is by far the largest migration of animals on the planet. They swim upwards from the twilight zone to the sunlight zone at night to feed under the cover of darkness, but then head back down to take advantage of anonymity in the gloom by day. Leading the nightly excursion is the microscopic zooplankton – the tiny animals that drift in the ocean currents. They rise up to graze on the phytoplankton. They are followed by small fish and squid, which, in turn, are tracked by bigger fish, which are hunted by the top predators, such as sharks.

One of the vertical migrants is the giant oarfish, the world's longest bony fish. In 1963, an oarfish estimated to be 15 metres long was seen by scientists off the New Jersey coast, but most specimens are shorter. The fish is ribbon-shaped, with a 'crown' of long, red fin rays on its head, giving rise to its other common English name 'king of the herrings'. It tends to swim vertically, with its head uppermost and its slender body almost invisible in the gloom. The undulations of the body match the dappled moonlight beaming down from above, making it tricky to see, and it takes advantage of the mass migration to the surface, preying upon the smaller vertical commuters. It feeds by sucking in zooplankton, such as shrimp-like krill and other crustaceans. Come the morning it heads back down and hides in the darkness of the twilight zone.

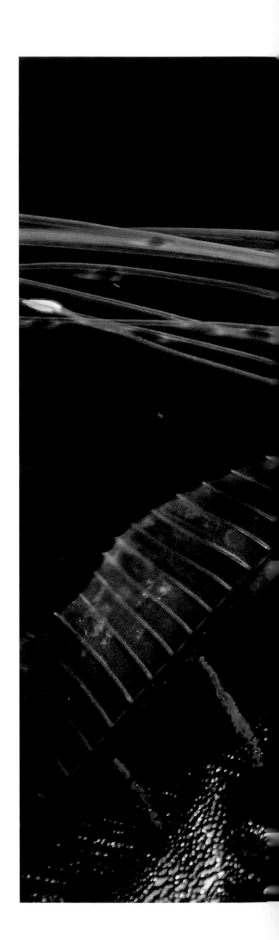

KING OF HERRINGS (right) The head of the oarfish is adorned with a 'crown' of fin rays.

'The dolphins push the shoals of lantern fish to the surface, and the sea begins to boil as these massive yellowfin tuna, each weighing over 100 kilograms, smash into the shoals.' MARK BROWNLOW, Series Producer

dive-bomb the bait ball. All are inadvertently helping each other with their waves of attack, but really it's mayhem, and as the fish leap clear of the surface to escape, the sea boils.

This is the tuna's strategy for surviving out here, but it was almost their downfall. Purse seine nets targeting tuna have regularly trapped spinner dolphins, and tens of thousands have been killed. However, changes in fishing regulations, which force fishermen to use nets from which the dolphins can escape, have brought the species back from the brink of extinction, and the numbers have now stabilised.

PORPOISING DOLPHINS (ABOVE)

A large pod of spinner dolphins is on the move. Each dolphin swims rapidly just below the surface, bursts into the air, and then drops back into the water to coast a short distance, before active swimming starts the cycle again. The moment in the air reduces the drag of the water, so the dolphin travels more efficiently.

While the back-down procedure might spare dolphins from being drowned or mangled in the winches, it is very stressful for a dolphin to be captured again and again. There are some estimates indicating that a dolphin might be caught and released on average eight times in one year. It was something that Mark and the film crew became very much aware.

'In the last few days, fishing boats homed in on our helicopter, recognising a shortcut to the tuna. We learned a sad truth from our guide Niko about the killing of spinner dolphins by the tuna fleets. Many are still killed, even after the implementation of tuna-friendly fishing techniques.'

World's Fastest

The most spectacular attacks must be those of the sailfish, reputed to be the world's fastest fish. It is one of the billfish, the group that includes swordfish and marlin, and it uses its 'sword' to slash at the shoal, disabling the baitfish and making them easy prey.

Forty or more can be involved in an attack, and before they make runs at a bait ball, they raise their great dorsal fin like a sail and change colour. Their normally silvery or brownish sides suddenly sport bold stripes and spots. It is all intended both to communicate their intentions and to intimidate the smaller fish, driving them into ever-tighter balls.

Off the Pacific coast of Costa Rica and in the Atlantic, close to the northeast tip of Mexico's Yucatan Peninsula, the clue that sailfish are hunting sardines is the telltale flock of keen-eyed frigate birds overhead. It has enabled researchers from the Billfish Research Project in Costa Rica and from European and US universities working off Cancun to find bait balls easily and make detailed observations of the fish's attack strategy – and they have discovered that it may not actually have one! Unlike dolphins, sailfish attacks do not appear to be coordinated, but they do take turns. One after another, and relatively slowly considering the speeds they can reach, each sailfish lunges into the school. Its bill is covered with tiny file-like micro-teeth, which help grip the prey, but although 95 per cent of these attacks result in injured fish, only a quarter land a mouthful of food.

Curiously, the sailfish actually eat fewer fish than if they were hunting alone, but by getting together they do not have to work so hard to catch them. It is an energy-efficient way to feed in the open ocean, and the scientists think that this taking-it-in-turns behaviour is a possible evolutionary forerunner to the more complex cooperative hunting strategies shown by other group-living animals, such as dolphins.

SWIMMING RAPIERS (right) A small group of sailfish corrals a bait ball of much smaller fish.

A Most Beautiful Shark

The blue shark follows its nose. This sleek transoceanic traveller is built to cover the most nautical miles for the least effort, for it is shaped like a glider, with a slender body and long pectoral fins that act like wings. On its lengthy migrations it swims towards the surface and then glides slowly down, repeating the pattern over and over again, an effective way to conserve energy. Shark scientists consider it to be the most beautiful of sharks, adapted perfectly for open ocean life. Its feeding strategy is simply to sniff out food, and it has the means to do so.

There are many extravagant claims for a shark's smelling ability, such as detecting blood in the water from over a mile away or a drop of fish oil in an Olympic-sized swimming pool, but much of this is untrue. Sharks'

BLUE DOG (below) The slender blue shark is found in both temperate and tropical seas all over the world, and travels vast distances around and across oceans.

sense of smell is certainly better than ours, and it varies between species, but the reality is that they can't smell anything like a drop in an Olympic-sized swimming pool, according to biologists at Florida Atlantic University, who have tested several types of sharks and rays. Even so, some species are able to detect one drop of scent in a billion drops of water, the equivalent of a drop of blood in a family-sized swimming pool. This is roughly the background concentration of amino acids and proteins dissolved in coastal waters. If they were adapted to detect smaller quantities, they would not be able to tell the difference between food and other random chemicals. In the open ocean, sharks like the blue shark could well detect lower concentrations because the background 'noise' is less.

Squid and small fish are regular foods, but the blue shark is an opportunist, alert to anything that triggers its senses, even creatures as small as krill, which it can 'filter' out with special structures on its gills. However, it increases its luck as it swims up and down, checking out currents at different depths for the whiff of anything remotely edible, using the structure of the ocean to its advantage. About a third of its brain is dedicated to interpreting odours, so it uses its heightened sense of smell to compare the strength of odours reaching its left and right nostrils. Then it follows the trail upstream to their source, like the floating carcass of a fin whale recently struck by a ship.

Blue sharks had been rumoured to scavenge on the bodies of whales and other marine mammals, and now the BBC crew has confirmation on film. The sharks swim slowly around the whale, their circle gradually tightening on every circuit, their senses probing the dead body for any sign of danger. Suddenly, the first shark takes a bite. It is the signal for the rest to pile in. They take huge mouthfuls, anchored by the stiletto-like teeth in their lower jaws, and then they shake their heads from side to side, enabling the triangular teeth in their upper jaws to slice off the fat and flesh. Unfortunately, their long snouts get in the way, so they have to point vertically upwards, their snouts sometimes out of the water. This behaviour has not seen before, but it is worth the effort. The blubber in particular is high-energy food, so the sharks feed upwards of eight hours until fully gorged. Such a meal can fuel them for many days afterwards, the digested fats and oils stored in their large livers for harder times ahead. It might also keep them out of trouble.

By feeding on the whale carcass, they are sated, so they are less likely to be attracted to bait put out by long-line fishermen. These people have a financial interest in those long fins, which are destined for the lucrative shark-fin soup market. Tens of millions of blue sharks are killed each year, even though their bodies are known to contain high levels of heavy metals, such as mercury and lead, a real risk to human health. Despite the health warning, their beautiful fins could still be the cause of their demise.

SMELL OF WHALE (opposite left) Guided by its nose, the blue shark is led to a dead fin whale still afloat at the surface.

WHALE OF A FEAST (opposite right) The shark circles the carcass to check it out before tucking in.

ENERGY-RICH BLUBBER (bottom) Its jaws are underslung and its snout is so long that the shark has difficulty tearing away the blubber.

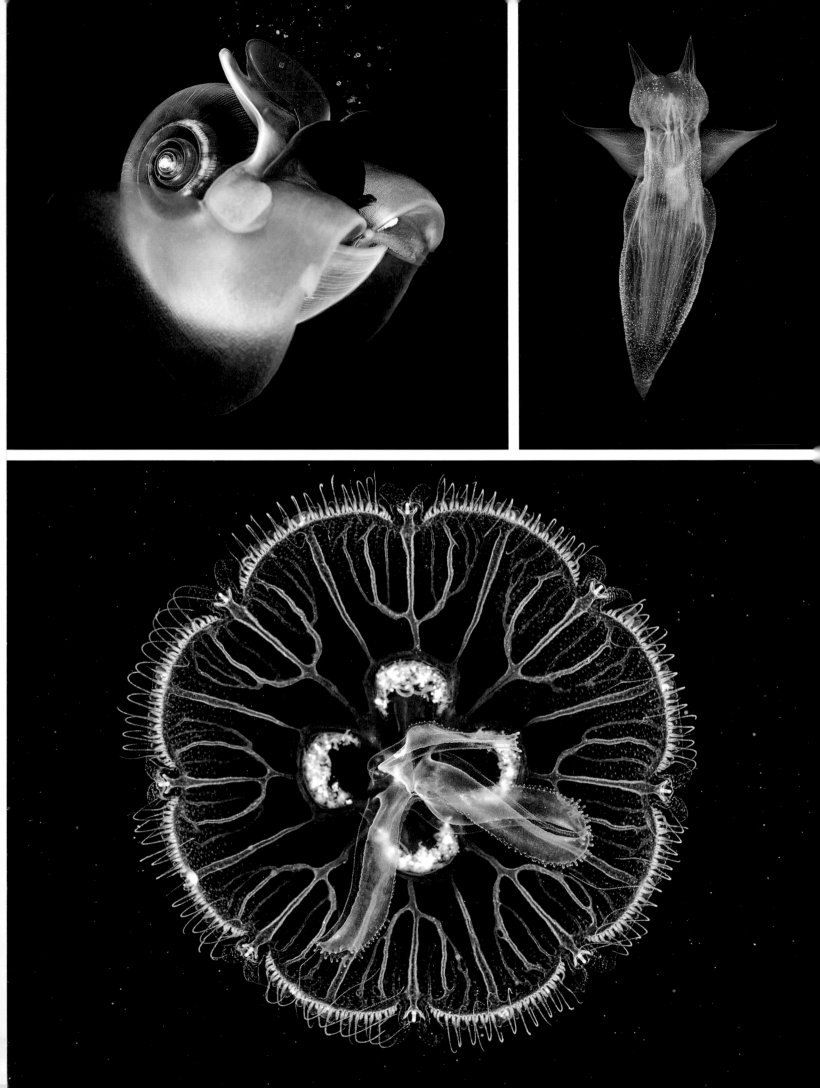

FLOATING JELLY (above) Jellyfish are roughly the same density as water so they do not sink, and they can swim upside down, as well as the right way up.

SEA BUTTERFLY (opposite top left) This little character is a swimming sea snail. Its foot is shaped as two lobes, and this propels it along.

SEA ANGEL (opposite top right) This is a swimming sea slug. It 'rows' with its 'wings' and catches sea butterflies.

MOON JELLY (opposite bottom) The moon jellyfish is so wispy and translucent that only its horseshoe-shaped gonads give it away.

from its nesting beach on Papua in the southwest Pacific to jellyfish-rich feeding areas off the coast of Oregon in the northeast Pacific, and was on its way back when its tracking signal was lost. Like all marine reptiles, they must surface to breathe and so a turtle's head popping out of the water might well be the source of many 'sea serpent' sightings in northern waters.

One notable jelly, not a true jellyfish but a siphonophore made up of four different organisms, has part of its body almost permanently above the surface. The notoriously painful Portuguese man o' war has a sail-like structure filled with gas. With this it can be blown along in the wind like a sailboat, so it is propelled by the wind as well as ocean currents. Below the sail are long tentacles, which generally reach to about 10 metres, but lengths of 30 metres have been known. They are armed with rows of stinging cells that can kill a fish on contact, so it may come as a surprise to find the imperial blackfish living amongst them, seemingly without a care. Whether it is immune or just very careful about what it bumps into is not clear, but it is certainly agile and not too fussy about what it hides under.

Imperial blackfish or medusa fish have been found under floating refrigerators and just about anything that does not sink. This behaviour is shown by many open ocean fish. They seek out anything floating at the surface and hide under it. It's a safe haven. One of the BBC production team saw several little fish hiding under a paintbrush, so a large wooden log is a big draw. It becomes the centre of an entire floating ecosystem.

Lost Years and a Log

The fallen bough, washed into the sea by a river or toppled from coastal cliffs, becomes encrusted with barnacles and algae, and young sea turtles come to feed on them. The log is their temporary life raft, and their presence here has solved a long-standing biological mystery. When turtle hatchlings leave their beach, they head out into the open ocean and are probably faced with the most challenging times of their life, what scientists have dubbed the 'lost years' because nobody knew where they went until they returned to lay eggs five years later. Now we know.

'We stumbled on the answer without fully realising it,' John Ruthven reveals. 'More than 160 kilometres off the coast of eastern Australia, with 3 kilometres of clear water below, we spotted a floating log. Diving below it, we found many creatures hiding, including a young hawksbill sea turtle – not little, not large, but middle-sized. This is probably where it spends its so-called 'lost years'.

'Scientists can trace the paths of small turtles like this using miniature satellite tags. They show that hatchling turtles go far out to sea, and temperature sensors on the tags reveal that the little reptiles keep warm and develop faster by staying close to the surface, sheltered by floating objects.

'After hatching, a baby turtle faces a daunting gauntlet of predators near the coast, and so it takes its chances on the high sea. When some inquisitive oceanic whitetip sharks came by, I wondered if this wasn't much of a choice, but anything a turtle can do to improve its one-in-a-thousand odds of reaching adulthood must be useful.'

The young sea turtles ride the ocean currents, like many young marine creatures, hiding beneath flotsam, jetsam, logs and rafts of floating seaweeds, such as those found in the Sargasso Sea, part of the North

OCEAN HIDING PLACE (below) A young sea turtle finds refuge amongst a floating mat of sargassum.

Atlantic Gyre. Here, drift lines of *Sargassum*, a type of brown seaweed kept afloat by airbladders, are host to their own specialist community of animals, like the sargassum crab and the exquisitely camouflaged sargassum fish. These are the preferred hiding places for young turtles, but these miniature hotspots also attract unwelcome guests, and the predators of the open ocean are amongst the most inquisitive, none more so than the oceanic whitetip shark, which John had seen prowling.

At the slightest hint of food, the oceanic whitetip swims in directly and without fear. It may not have fed for weeks, so it wastes no time. It prefers fish to turtles, so an attack would be an exception, but there is another large and dangerous species with chainsaw-like teeth that would make easy work of a young sea turtle's shell, and it deliberately targets these ocean drifters. It's the tiger shark, thought until recently to be mainly a coastal species. However, tagging studies have shown that tiger sharks from the Caribbean head out a short distance into the Atlantic each summer in search of young, naïve and easy-to-catch loggerhead turtles.

Garbage Patch Ocean

At one time, the debris in which young sea turtles hide was mainly natural, but nowadays a flood of plastics dominates. It is thought that the equivalent of a large garbage-truck-load of plastic is dumped into the sea every minute of every day. The effects are an ecological nightmare.

Thousands of sea turtles are either strangled by discarded nylon fishing gear or choke on plastic bags, mistaking them for jellyfish. It is estimated that over half of living turtles have eaten plastic at some time in their life, and about 90 per cent of seabirds have consumed plastic particles that they have mistaken for food. Some starve to death because they feel full after eating plastic debris, and they consume it because they are duped. Albatrosses, petrels and shearwaters in the open ocean are guided by their keen sense of smell, and the odour of rotting algae that collects on plastic, similar to the pong of boiled cabbage, tricks the birds into consuming it. Scientists studying albatross nesting sites on oceanic islands frequently find birds dead, the result of the plastics they have consumed at sea clogging their intestines.

STOMACH CONTENTS (below) A pile of plastic is all that remains after the walls of the bird's stomach have rotted away. It probably died of starvation, due to a blocked gut.

PLASTIC JELLYFISH (opposite top)
A green sea turtle mistakes a clear plastic bag for a jellyfish off the coast of Tenerife.

And it is not only visible pieces of plastic that are a problem. When plastic is degraded by sunlight and ground down by wave action into micro-particles, the grazers in the zooplankton consume the invisible plastic soup, so it enters the food chain and is concentrated in the animals higher up the chain. Although it passes through the gut of predators, the concern is that the plastic particles unload their burden of toxic chemicals as they pass through the intestines, and these concentrate in the animal's flesh, ultimately coming back to haunt seafood lovers. It is now thought that in places like the centre of the North Pacific Gyre, which is poor in nutrients, there are six times more plastic particles than plankton, and that some fish are eating it in preference to their natural food, poisoning entire ecosystems, including those that end with us. We are yet to fully understand the consequences.

Seamount Central

A fundamental need for mid-ocean travellers, whether they be simple jellyfish or sophisticated whales, is to know where they are and in which direction they should be going. We have magnetic compasses and GPS, and marine life is not so very different, except that it relies on a special 'sixth sense' that detects the Earth's magnetic field. Even jellyfish seem to have it.

Many animals are thought to orientate to and navigate by the magnetic field, with geological features, such as seamounts, having their own distinctive magnetic signatures. Humpback, fin, blue and northern right whales have been tracked travelling from one seamount to the next. For them, the ocean is far from featureless. As long as they have a 'geomagnetic mental map', a seamount becomes their navigation beacon.

In fact, seamounts and volcanic islands feature strongly in the lives of mid-ocean animals. They use them as dormitories, nurseries, meeting places and feeding sites. Large schools of scalloped hammerhead sharks, for example, rest by them. They swim aimlessly back and forth during the day, before individuals peel off in the evening to go hunting. Spinner dolphins in Hawaii show a similar daily pattern.

Underwater mountains deflect deep-sea currents, pulling up nutrients from the bottom of the sea, so their surrounding waters are rich in marine life. Around the Canary Islands, shortfin pilot whales have become so enamoured with the ample food supply that they have become residents, rearing their calves here year round.

BEREAVED MOTHER (below) A mother pilot whale appears to mourn her dead calf floating at the surface, possibly a victim of toxic shock caused by plastics or plastics related chemicals in her milk. A blue shark and tuna wait for her to leave so they can feed on the body.

HAMMERHEAD SCHOOL (overleaf) Hundreds of scalloped hammerhead sharks gather off Darwin's Arch in the Galápagos Islands. During the day they swim aimlessly back and forth, as if resting. At dusk, the school splits up and the sharks hunt during the night, returning to the island by dawn.

Pinpoint Navigation

Whale sharks adopt volcanic islands as nursery sites, finding them by using that special sixth sense. Sharks in the eastern Pacific, for example, pitch up at Darwin's Arch in the Galápagos archipelago. It is hardly more than a rock, and from June until November on average 1,200 gigantic whale sharks appear, and almost all look to be pregnant.

Scientists believe that the whale sharks find this tiny dot in the ocean guided by electroreceptors in pores in their snout. They detect electrical fields in the ocean currents that are induced by the geomagnetic field. With this, whale sharks pinpoint the tiny islet with considerable accuracy; if they were out by a couple of degrees, they would miss it, but Darwin, like all volcanic islands, has its own signature of strong and weak magnetic fields. They radiate outwards from the island, providing ocean travellers with a magnetic street map, and Darwin's Arch is like a roundabout on the Eastern Pacific magnetic highway.

A female's distended belly is an indication she could be pregnant, and that up to 300 baby whale sharks are waiting to be born. It is an odd place to give birth, for there are many large predators here, including tiger sharks, but she dives down the side of the volcano accompanied by smaller silky sharks. A BBC onboard camera, similar to those attached to the sperm whales, has monitored her progress for the very first time. It shows smaller silky sharks swooping in to rub their bodies against her rough skin, possibly to divest themselves of external parasites. It is a common enough occurrence, but what the BBC's camera recorded came as a shock to viewing scientists. Every time a silky came close, there was a strange roaring sound. It was the first time that anybody had witnessed such a thing, and nobody has a clue what it is.

However, as she drops ever deeper, the other sharks leave her. She is thought to give birth at some point down in the deep, although nobody has actually witnessed it. The rocks and submarine canyons of the island have many places for youngsters to hide and, having carried out her maternal duties, the mother disappears into the big blue just as quickly and mysteriously as she arrived, her camera popping back to the surface a few days later.

WHALE SHARK NURSERY (left) A heavily pregnant whale shark arrives in the Galápagos Islands, where it is thought she will give birth.

Ultimate Sacrifice

While whales and sharks cross the oceans below the waves, seabirds embark on breathtaking journeys above. The wandering albatross circumnavigates the stormy Southern Ocean up to four times a year, and does not touch terra firma for the best part of two years between bouts at the nest.

Carried on her long, narrow glider-like wings, spanning more than 3 metres – the longest of any bird – a female albatross may have flown over 900 kilometres a day, much of it without flapping, just using the wind. Now she returns to breed, possibly for the very last time. Seeking out her long-term partner in the sprawling colony of 800–900 pairs on remote Bird Island, at the northwest tip of South Georgia in the South Atlantic, she sets about bringing up her single chick. Wandering albatross numbers have fallen in recent years because birds consume plastics or are caught by long-line fishermen, so every chick counts.

When the pair reunites, the excitement is clear to see. The birds stretch their necks to the sky, open their wings and dance.

'They make the most unusual almost scream-like sounds, as well as vibrating their beak so it clacks rapidly when they throw their heads back,' recalls Lucy Quinn, one of British Antarctic Survey's zoologists on Bird Island.

It's hard not to be moved by the affection the birds show to each other, but more pragmatically, this bond they show so openly has enabled them to rear twenty chicks during their long lives. Most wandering albatrosses live

OLD FRIENDS UNITE (above) Pairs of wandering albatrosses are lifelong partners. After months apart at sea, they greet each other and establish old bonds with a spectacular dance.

SOARING THE SOUTHERN OCEAN (opposite) Wandering albatrosses embark on fishing trips of 10,000 kilometres for up to 20 days, yet so efficient are they at soaring that they use little more energy than when they are at the nest.

for about 50 years, but this pair is now in its mid-forties, and this will be one of the last times they mate.

Scientists from the British Antarctic Survey know most of their story because they have been monitoring them and many other pairs on Bird Island for nearly 60 years. They have compiled the longest ever dataset on any species of animal in the world, and they have discovered something quite remarkable. They knew that this would be one of the birds' last chicks because as they entered their twilight years, their breeding activity declined. However, this was followed by a dramatic increase in breeding success because of an increase in parental investment at their final breeding attempt. The ageing female and her partner were forced to fly and gather food like never before, travelling several thousand miles for each meal, and this inevitably took its toll. For some reason, the old albatrosses gave their last chick the best chance of surviving. How they knew they were going to die and this was their last chance to breed is another of nature's mysteries.

HUNGRY GIANT (below) With its thick down, the growing wandering albatross chick looks even bigger than its parents. It will remain in the nest for 9 months.

ALBATROSS SURVEY (opposite) Lucy Quinn of the British Antarctic Survey and one of her study birds

'**If you are beside them when they hold their wings out and dance, you can feel the air whoosh as they bring up their impressive wings.**'

LUCY QUINN, Zoologist

A Great Gathering

Off the northwest coast of Sri Lanka, an even bigger surprise met scientists studying the behaviour of sperm whales. Like those off Dominica, sperm whales in the Indian Ocean live in small groups, and, as they show a strong fidelity to a local area for feeding and social interactions, whales from different localities generally do not mix. Sperm whales in Sri Lanka, for example, are quite separate from those in the Maldives or Mauritius. Imagine, then, the astonishment of whale watchers when up to 300 sperm whales in many groups appear off Sri Lanka, and researcher Yoland Bosiger was there to witness the unusual event.

'Underwater cameramen Dan Beecham and Didier Noirot slipped silently into the water, and, with engines in neutral, we waited. More than twenty sperm whales swam towards them, so we knew we would get some fantastic shots, but then the whales changed direction, and, before we knew it, they had completely surrounded our small boat. The whales were so close that I could have reached out and touched them with my hand.'

Dan, meanwhile, was right in amongst the whales. 'At times I was surrounded by whales, to my left, to my right, and underneath me. The clicks of so many whales communicating with each other was so loud and powerful, I could actually feel the sound reverberating through my body.'

This intense chattering that Dan had experienced could be the whale equivalent of the cocktail party or family get together. These mass gatherings might well be major 'cultural' events in the sperm whale calendar. Just as human culture passes on things like language and tastes in food, whales and dolphins are probably doing the same. The Sri Lankan whales could be swapping stories about the best places to hunt or perhaps this patch of sea is a rendezvous site where whales meet the opposite sex. Nobody really knows, but what is clear to Shane Gero in Dominica is that sound dominates the lives of these giants.

'In the darkness of the deep ocean, their world is a world of sound. They see with sound. They hunt with sound. They navigate and communicate with sound. As visual animals, it's hard for us to picture what life is like beneath the surface.'

Off Sri Lanka, large males shadow and almost dwarf the females, and it is rare to see so many family groups in one place. Whatever the reason, sperm whales appear to have the ultimate solution to survival in the big blue – an amazing natural sonar system, exceptional social intelligence and communication, and diverse local cultures that are filled with traditional solutions for success.

GOING TO THE BALL (below) Sperm whales are usually seen in small family groups, but occasionally families get together and then there's a big party.

That sperm whales are in our oceans at all is remarkable. Whaling fleets targeted them for the spermaceti oil in their great heads until as recently as the 1980s. Today, people continue to be a major threat, and this is critically important because rich and complex lives are at stake, a multicultural community of open ocean nomads we hardly know.

'Sperm whales have lived in parallel to us for generations,' Shane Gero points out, 'even longer than humans have walked upright. While we have put people on the Moon and robots on Mars, the deep open ocean home of the sperm whale is still largely unknown. These enormous aggregations off Sri Lanka are one of the largest and most puzzling underwater spectacles on Earth. They are a brief glimpse into their way of life in a part of our shared planet that is difficult for us to even explore.'

'At times I was surrounded by whales, to my left, to my right, and underneath me. The clicks of so many whales communicating with each other was so loud and powerful, I could actually feel the sound reverberating through my body.' DAN BEECHAM, Cameraman

A GREAT GATHERING (above) Underwater cameraman Didier Noirot dives amongst the sperm whale aggregations off the coast of Sri Lanka in the Indian Ocean.

chapter six
The Deep

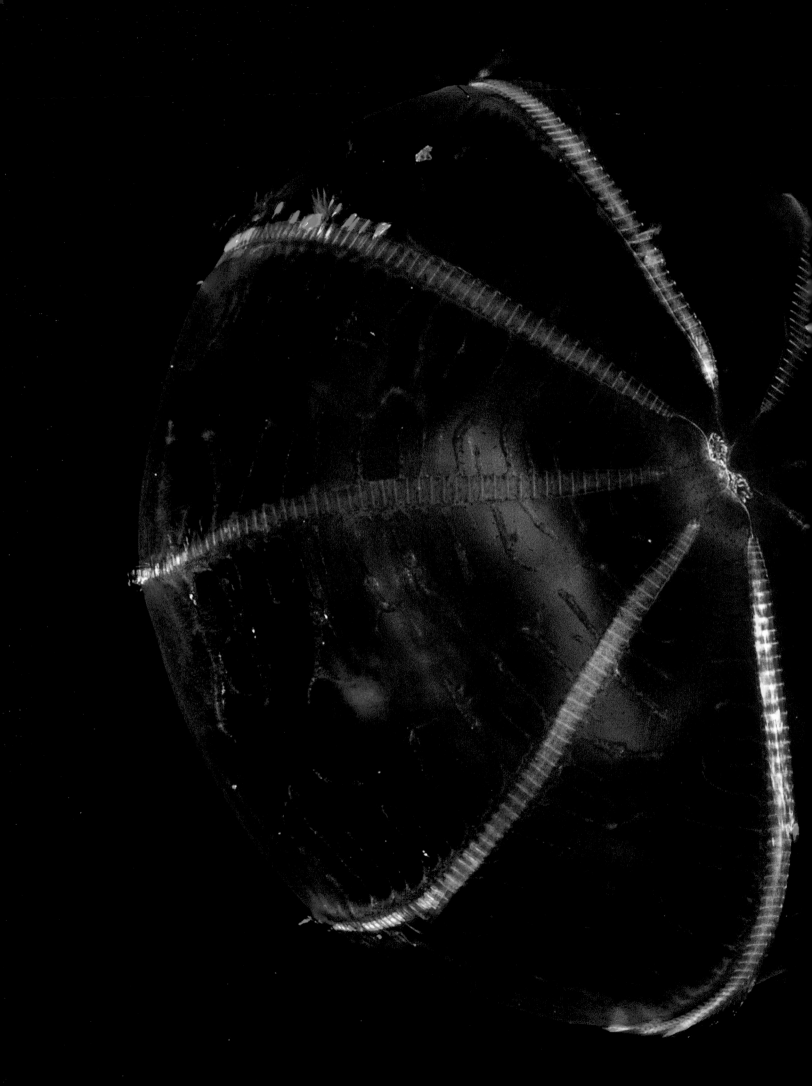

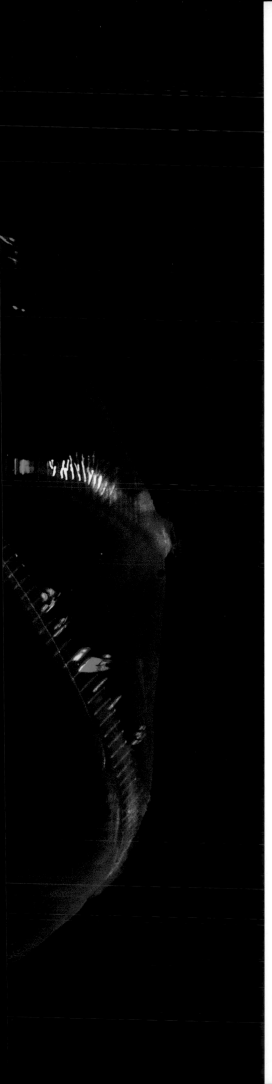

CIGAR COMB JELLY (left) Ctenophores or comb jellies are the largest non-colonial animals to swim with cilia (motile hairs). The colours are not bioluminescence, but are caused by the scattering of light as the cilia move.

TRANSLUCENT OCTOPUS (previous page) This new species of octopus was discovered in deep waters in the Arctic. It has yet to be named.

Deep below the surface of the ocean is an eerie and mysterious world that remains largely unexplored and has been completely hidden until recent times. Beyond the reach of sunlight and under unimaginable pressure, it is hard to understand how life could survive in such a place, yet it is the largest living space in the ocean, home maybe to more species than in all the other marine habitats combined... but nobody knows for sure.

Twelve people have walked on the Moon, but only three have been to the bottom of the ocean's deepest deep – the Challenger Deep. We have better maps of the surface of Mars than we do of our own seabed. But all of this is changing. The deep sea may have been a no-go area for humanity in the past, but now we have the 'spaceships' to explore inner space, including fresh eyes with which to pierce the inky depths. We have manned and remote-controlled deep-sea submersibles that can withstand great pressures, and we have developed new sampling techniques and made advances in camera platforms and image capture. All of these are revealing that the deep sea is stocked full of surprises, even if not all are welcome.

Some of the more disquieting discoveries were soft drinks cans at 2,300 metres in the Cayman Trough, a plastic shopping bag next to a deep-sea vent in the Pacific, and food packaging 1,000 kilometres from the nearest land and 1,500 metres deep in the middle of the Atlantic Ocean. On almost every ground-breaking dive, scientists in deep-sea submersibles are finding human litter all over the ocean, even in the deepest parts. Our trash has reached Earth's final frontier long before we have.

Cold Beginnings

Antarctica is the coldest, driest and windiest place on Earth, so it might seem an odd place to begin the story of the deep sea, but evidence is mounting that the ancestors of life forms found in the abyss today lived on the fringes of the southern continent in the past.

For one thing, the Antarctic's inshore waters are unusual. The weight of the polar ice sheet has pushed down the entire continent so the continental shelf is considerably deeper than any other. The shelf is generally 500–600 metres deep at its outer edge, compared to 100–200 metres elsewhere in the world, and there are deep canyons, some more than 1,000 metres deep. These are carved out by powerful turbidity currents that rush down the continental slope like avalanches, picking up sediments and increasing in speed as they go. It means conditions here are not so different to those in parts of the deep sea, and it has led scientists to suggest that Antarctica's continental shelf could be a gateway between these two underwater worlds.

In the Antarctic, the seawater temperature can drop to around minus 2°C before the sea freezes solid. It was not always this way, however: the climate was once subtropical. Then, after the breakup of the supercontinent Gondwana, Antarctica separated from the other continents and its climate cooled, culminating in the opening of the Drake Passage, between the Antarctic Peninsula and the tip of South America, about 23 million years ago. This allowed the Antarctic Circumpolar Current to flow and Antarctica was effectively isolated from the warmer parts of the ocean. It became a 'frozen continent' and the swing in climate triggered huge changes in the populations of animals living off its shores.

Fish, for example, cannot cope when their tissues freeze at minus 0.8°C, and crabs and lobsters are unable to regulate their magnesium levels, so there are few species in Antarctic waters even to this day. For the fish, this meant a gradual population shift, over millions of years, from species unable to exist in the cold to fish that had evolved the wherewithal to survive here.

The Antarctic ice dragon, for one, has antifreeze in its blood but no red blood cells. It looks like a ghost fish. However, blood without corpuscles flows more easily in the cold, and the colder the water the higher its oxygen content, so the icefish doesn't really need them anyway. Enough oxygen dissolves in the fluid of its blood to keep it alive. It and its toothfish relatives probably evolved from sluggish, bottom-dwelling fish, probably with normal blood, which evolved exceptional capabilities to be able to live in this challenging new habitat.

DEATH STAR (opposite left) The giant Antarctic sunstar catches krill on its many curled up arms. The little cod icefish waits to steal its prey.

ICEFISH (opposite right) Sir James Clark Ross first saw the Antarctic ice dragon during an expedition to the Antarctic (1839–1843). Unfortunately, before it could be properly described, the ship's cat ate it.

FLYING FEATHER DUSTER (opposite bottom) Seen from *Alucia*'s submersibles, this delicate feather star is swimming using the feathery fringes on its arms to help it rise up into the water column.

'**We were caught in blizzards of marine snow so thick that if we rested on the seabed the acrylic dome of the submersible was covered in a thick, white layer. It was like sitting in a snow globe.**' ORLA DOHERTY, Producer

Toothfish, like many of the resident predators here, are slow movers, relying on stealth and ambush to secure a meal. Scientists speculate that the ice dragon, for example, remains motionless on the seabed, propped up by the tripod created by its exceptionally long pectoral fin rays and its tail, in a similar way to the deep-sea tripod fish on the abyssal plain. It doesn't chase anything; instead, it waits for prey to pass by, the fish's sedentary lifestyle enabling it to avoid expending energy unnecessarily.

The scarcity of fish means that invertebrates dominate these waters; in fact, the seabed here has some of the densest populations of marine invertebrates on the planet. It is packed with brittle stars, sea stars, feather stars, sea anemones, sea cucumbers, cup corals, soft corals, tunicates and countless species of marine worms, along with deep-sea jellyfish and cold-adapted octopuses, these invertebrates accounting for the best part of the 8,200 recognised species living here. For *Blue Planet II* producer Orla Doherty, aboard a manned submersible, it was a breathtaking, if sometimes daunting, experience.

'Nothing prepared us for what we found – an abundance of life on the seafloor rivalling that on a coral reef. There was a sumptuous carpet of life, a riot of colour, unrivalled by any other location we had dived during the past two-and-a-half years.

WHITE CLIFF (above) *Alucia*'s manned submersible *Deep Rover* approaches the vertical walls of an enormous iceberg off the Antarctic Peninsula.

'On that first day, we were engulfed by a swarm of krill, which was drawn to our lights. There were so many, our pilot struggled to see where we were going. We switched off the lights, hoping they would disperse, and we were treated to something I never expected to see. All around us was a sea of pulsing blue lights – bioluminescent krill, the first time it had been observed like this in the wild, and something we were able to capture for the programme with our specialist low-light cameras.'

Food for all of these creatures trickles down from above – the moulted skins and dead bodies of krill, debris from the phytoplankton, and faeces from humpback whales that come here to feed each summer, tempted by the ocean's richness. Indeed, in summer, the first thing that strikes scientists who have been studying this area is the overwhelming amount of this 'marine snow', as it is known, another Antarctic experience for Orla and her crew.

'We were caught in blizzards of marine snow so thick that if we rested on the seabed the acrylic dome of the submersible was covered in a thick, white layer. It was like sitting in a snow globe.'

Feeding on the blizzard are colourful featherstars. These wispy crinoids, whose ancestors first appeared in the fossil record 480 million years ago, resemble living feather dusters. They wave their delicate arms to rise up in the water column, drift in the current and then sink gently once more to the seabed, always in search of the best places to intercept the snow, and they are very effective at catching it. Tiny tube feet guide food particles into a gutter that runs along each arm, where hair-like cells waft them towards the mouth, which, unlike sea stars, is on the upper side of their body.

The incredibly dense swarms of Antarctic krill, mysids and amphipods are food for myriad sea creatures, one of the largest being a giant sea star, about 60 centimetres across. This voracious species of sun star lives on the seabed, where it is such an efficient predator that the production team gave it the nickname 'death star'. It can have up to fifty arms, ten times more than the average starfish, and it curls them up, holding them away from the seabed so they are like fishing rods. They snag passing krill and small fish, which they grab with tiny pincers that snap shut when something brushes past them. The food is then passed towards the mouth, which is on the underside of the central disc.

The delicate and vulnerable featherstars are so prolific in these waters and the death star is able to hold up its arms without being attacked simply because there are so few fish to nibble on them; in fact, the dearth of fish means that the death star is one of the top predators, but it does not get everything its own way. A chubby little cod icefish, one of the few fish species that lives here, sneaks in to steal the catch from right out of its mouth.

Through the Gateway

'Giant' is a word frequently used by biologists to describe the creatures living on the Antarctic's continental shelf, for many species grow to exceptional sizes, a phenomenon known as 'polar gigantism'. There are sponges 2 metres tall that are thought to be hundreds of years old, and marine isopods – giant relatives of woodlice or pill bugs – that are 10 centimetres long, many times larger than their more familiar land-living relatives. The sea spiders are an arachnophobe's nightmare. They look like spiders, but they are actually pycnogonids. Some have a leg span of more than 40 centimetres and are festooned with Antarctic leeches.

It is this prevalence of larger-than-normal organisms that provides scientists with a hint that the Antarctic and the deep sea have an evolutionary link. In the similar near-freezing conditions at the bottom of the deep ocean there are even bigger isopods, such as the deep-sea giant isopod that grows to 76 centimetres long, an example of 'deep-sea gigantism', a feature shown by those other charismatic monsters of the deep – the colossal squid in cold Antarctic waters and the giant squid in the deep sea.

COLD WATER OCTOPUS (above)
Alucia's submersible tracks down an octopus able to survive in the icy cold Antarctic waters.

However, the animal revealing to scientists a more direct connection between the two domains is not a squid or an isopod, but an octopus. The octopus is known to have lived on the coast of the Antarctic about 33 million years ago, and its closest living relatives still live here today. Biologists have compared their DNA with that of as many deep-sea octopuses as they can find, and they have discovered that the ancestry of many of the deep-sea octopuses can be traced back to that early Antarctic octopus. They have also worked out how its descendants might have migrated to their new homes.

When Antarctica moved away from South America and the Drake Passage opened, the newly formed continent cooled significantly. Today, very cold and powerful winds blow off the continent, freezing the water and pushing it offshore as ice. The water beneath is cold, more salty and rich in oxygen, and, as it is denser than the rest of the ocean, it sinks, forming the descending limb of the southern hemisphere's part of the global ocean conveyor belt. Several million years ago, the thermohaline expressway, as the descending limb is sometimes known, started to flow from the Antarctic into the deep sea, and it still does today.

At that time, there was little oxygen in the deep sea, and so very little lived there, but riding on the expressway were animals from the Antarctic, including the octopuses. In this gateway between the Antarctic and the deep sea, toothfish had evolved the wherewithal to remain, while the octopuses were moving out, and about 15 million years ago the leavers began to spread northwards, throughout the world's oceans.

This flow continues to this day, at least, for now. This dense, oxygen-rich water from the Antarctic, together with similar currents from the surface to the deep-sea floor in the North Atlantic, carries the oxygen for much deep-sea life – the 'lungs of the deep'. Should our warming climate cause less of the ocean to freeze in winter, though, the flow of oxygen will weaken. What happens in the Antarctic (and the Arctic) determines the fate of deep-sea animals all around the world.

Recently, scientists estimated that the amount of oxygen in the oceans has declined by 2 per cent over the past five decades. There may be less oxygen in shallow waters, where surface waters are warming, because warmer water has less oxygen dissolved in it. In deeper waters, however, the decline in oxygen may be a sign that the life-giving flow of water from polar regions to the deep sea could already be weakening.

SEA SPIDER (below) An Antarctic pycnogonid is picked out by the submersible's lights and cameras, and the pictures fed to the *Alucia*.

Zoning of the Deep

Faced with such a vast body of water, scientists studying the deep sea divide it up conveniently into zones, each zone characterised by its depth, salinity, temperature and the amount (or lack) of light that reaches it. We are all familiar with shimmering sunlight reflecting off the sea's surface. This lends its name to the ocean's uppermost layer – the sunlight zone. But even here the water begins to play tricks with the light. A submersible crew will notice that the red component has largely been absorbed at a depth of less than 2 metres, followed by orange and yellow a little further down, leaving blues and greens. By 100 metres conditions turn distinctly gloomy, and little light penetrates beyond the 200-metre mark, the upper boundary of the first major zone of the deep sea. This is the twilight zone, where animals have goggle eyes, or gaping, fang-filled jaws, or you can see right through them.

PENETRATING SUNLIGHT (above) If conditions are right, sunlight may travel down as far as 1,000 metres deep, but there is rarely any significant light below 200 metres.

Down here, photosynthesis using energy from the Sun is no longer a viable means of manufacturing food. There is simply not enough light. Only 1 per cent of sunlight penetrates to these depths. There are no primary producers – the plants and plant-like organisms, such as phytoplankton, normally at the bottom of the food chain – so twilight zone animals depend entirely on those living at the surface. Some scavenge on their dead bodies and waste, such as mucus, faecal pellets and diatom shells, which sink down from above as marine snow, while others hunt the animals that make the daily vertical migration to the surface to feed at night and are back again by morning.

Big Eyes

This daily movement of animals makes the twilight zone an especially dynamic part of the ocean, a transitional layer between the surface and the abyss. Familiar animals visit from above, while strange creatures hide in the gloom.

A swordfish hunts down here in near darkness because its large eyes and brain are kept 10–15°C warmer than the surrounding seawater, and a sperm whale passes through the twilight zone on its way to and from the deep in pursuit of deep-sea squid, but the diminutive glass squid is a twilight resident.

The glass squid is well adapted to mid-water living. Its body fluids are laced with just the right amount of low-density ammonia solution to prevent it from sinking down or floating up, and it is almost transparent, so it is difficult to see. Only a flattened digestive gland – similar to a human liver – makes a shadow, and even this has a light organ at one end to help break up its outline.

Some glass squid also have very large eyes. There may be little light down here, but eyes are designed to pick up every last photon. A distant relative – the cock-eyed squid – has a normal-sized right eye that looks downwards to see predators approaching and an enormous left eye that permanently looks up to spot the silhouettes of prey against the surface. Some eyes are even more peculiar.

The tube-eye is a fish with tubular eyes, shaped like a pair of binoculars. Its super-sensitive vision enables it to pick out the tiny copepods on which it feeds. Catching the little crustaceans, however, is not so easy. They can jump away a few millimetres at high speed, their strongest leaps reaching velocities of nearly 1,000 body lengths per second, and that is in a medium as viscous as water, the equivalent of humans jumping through molasses. Copepods, it seems, could be the fastest and strongest animals on Earth, but the tube-eye is not defeated. Its tubular jaws shoot out and its oral cavity expands to 40 times its normal size, sucking in the copepods before they jump again.

The barreleye fish or spookfish is another oddball. It has swivelling eyes that can face forwards or look directly upwards through its transparent, fluid-filled, dome-shaped forehead. It is thought to filch the prey trapped by siphonophores that work the ocean like living drift nets. The siphonophore catches prey by attracting it towards its stinging cells by flashes of light. The barreleye picks up these flashes, and then drifts in and steals the siphonophore's hard-earned meal, its eyes protected from sting cells by its jelly-like forehead.

GLASS SQUID (opposite left) These swollen-bodied, small-tentacled translucent squid have a large chamber filled with an ammonia solution, which aids buoyancy. It led to them being called 'bathyscaphoid squid' because they are shaped like a bathyscaphe. Their transparency is a form of camouflage that affords them some protection.

TUBE-EYE (opposite right) The body of this elongated fish is no more than 28 centimetres long, but its strange, whip-like tail fin triples the overall length. Its head has a pair of tube-shaped eyes that resemble a pair of binoculars. It is distantly related to cod and hake, but has been assigned an order all of its own, the Stylephoriformes.

BARREL-EYE (bottom) The clear shield that protects the barreleye's eyes was discovered by scientists at Monterey Aquarium Research Institute. They were the first to film this extraordinary fish in its native habitat.

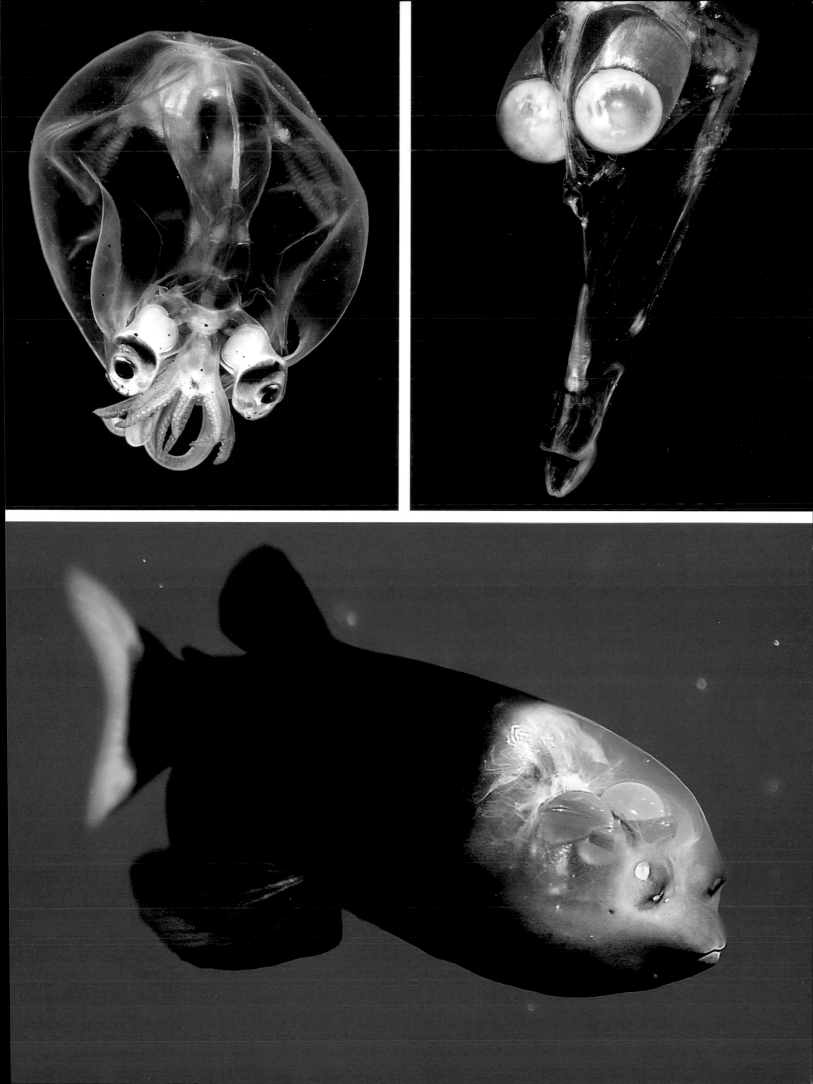

Invisibility Cloak

The small amount of light that reaches the twilight zone has the potential to reveal the whereabouts of the animals trying to hide here. Seen from below they would be silhouetted against the surface, so they take measures to disguise or break up their outline with rows of photophores or light organs on the undersides of their bodies. The light they emit blends in with the glow from the surface, a process known as counter-illumination, rendering the fish or squid almost invisible when viewed from underneath.

The ubiquitous lanternfish family has light organs along its flanks, and the light from them can be controlled so they match that coming from the surface, masking the fish's silhouette. The pattern is different in different species, indicating they could also be used for communication during shoaling and maybe even courtship. One species of lanternfish has large 'headlights' close to each eye, which could be used to attract and light up prey, and some have light organs on the tail that might be used as false lures to confuse potential predators.

FANGTOOTH (below) The fangtooth is only 16 centimetres long, but its jaws are filled with huge teeth. Its two bottom front teeth are so long, it has sockets on either side of its brain to accommodate them when its mouth is closed.

LANTERNFISH (above) This lanternfish has huge eyes and forward-pointing light organs, which gives rise to its alternative name – headlight fish.

One of those hunters is the fangtooth, a deep-sea fish that has been seen at depths down to 5,000 metres. It has the biggest teeth for its body size of any fish, yet, for all its apparent ferocity it seems to rely on luck more than anything else to bump into dinner. It lacks good eyesight, so it cannot clearly see a lanternfish's light signals; instead, its main sense appears to be an especially well-developed lateral line that picks up movements and vibrations in the water, and when it makes contact, it has a keen sense of smell to establish whether it is edible or not.

Even more formidable are shoals of Humboldt squid. With a body length of up to 2 metres, it is one the world's larger species of squid, and one of the most ferocious. Spanish fishermen call them *diablo rojo* ('red devils') because they flash red and white as they hunt. They migrate vertically each day, following the lanternfish to the surface at night. As they jet about, they appear to 'flash talk', with changing colour patterns on their skin. Whether they are communicating is unknown, but thirty or forty individuals spiral up together below a shoal of lanternfish. They grab prey by extending their two long tentacles in less than a second. Between 100 and 200 suckers on the club-like ends are rimmed with razor-like teeth, so nothing is likely to escape. A sharp, parrot-like beak rips into flesh, but it is thought they do not have the biting strength to sever bone. Even so, they have been known to attack divers near the surface and have put underwater cameras out of action.

Climate Change Allies

Light may be in short supply in the twilight zone, but animals are most certainly not. Scientists have estimated that more than 90 per cent of the ocean's fish biomass lives here. According to a recent study published in the scientific journal *Nature*, it amounts to more than 10 billion tonnes, which is one hundred times the world's annual fish catch and two hundred times the existing biomass of chickens, considered to be the most numerous vertebrate on land. It means these twilight fish probably play a role in the sequestering of carbon dioxide from the atmosphere. Phytoplankton at the surface use carbon dioxide to manufacture food, and they are consumed by zooplankton. These tiny animals, in turn, are food for the twilight zone fish that swim up to the surface at night to feed. The carbon goes into building bodies, and when the fish die, their bodies sink down into the deep sea, taking the carbon with them, although only about 1 per cent reaches the seabed, most having been recycled by other animals that intercept it on the way down. It makes them key allies against the threats of man-made climate change, yet commercial fishing fleets are beginning to target them as other fish stocks closer to the surface are fished out – another carbon sink lost.

JUMBO SQUID (above) The Humboldt or jumbo squid was once found only in warm waters off the Pacific coast of Central America. It is now appearing as far north as Alaska, and south to Tierra del Fuego. Warming waters due partly to El Niño and the overfishing of predatory competitors has enabled it to migrate into new areas.

Where the Sun Never Shines

ALARM JELLY (above) The deep-sea Atolla jellyfishes are bioluminescent, especially the ring of gonads in the middle of the jellyfish. They flash with a bright blue light when the jellyfish is threatened.

The demarcation line between the bottom of the twilight zone and the zone directly below is at a depth of 1,000 metres. Below this is a dark and even more mystifying void – the midnight zone, which extends down to 4,000 metres. There is no sunlight at all down here. Living organisms are the main sources of light. Some generate their own light, others borrow that of symbiotic, bioluminescent bacteria, and the light they emit is generally a blue-green colour. It can have any one of several functions – to see or confuse prey, scare aggressors, attract a partner or something to eat, or talk to the neighbours. The 'alarm' jellyfish, for example, hoodwinks an assailant with a series of startlingly bright flashes, while at the same time drawing in other predators that hopefully attack and see off the attacker.

The viperfish attracts small midnight zone animals to its mouth with a bright light on a short 'fishing rod', an extension of the first spine on its dorsal fin. Its huge fang-like teeth grab any inquisitive fish, squid or shrimp that approaches too closely. However, its teeth are so big that if it should get its attack wrong, it is in danger of impaling itself.

One of the deep-sea dragonfish goes one step further. The stoplight loosejaw has an unusual trick up its sleeve should its prey try diversionary tactics. When stalking a deep-sea shrimp, a bright blue bioluminescent smokescreen can suddenly blow up in its face. It is an escape behaviour exhibited by many deep-sea shrimps, but this particular dragonfish counters with its own bioluminescence. It turns on its special red light and illuminates a small search area. It is one of the few creatures in the deep sea that can see red. It also has chlorophyll in its eyes to boost the colour range of its vision. Green plants and algae generally use the molecule for photosynthesis, but this fish is the only animal known to employ it for a different purpose.

The dragonfish's red beam travels a short distance, as the colour red is rapidly absorbed, so there are many animals here that are coloured either red or black. It makes them difficult to see. Deep-sea shrimps are red (even before they're boiled), and the dragonfish's stomach is opaque black so that other predators cannot see any bioluminescent prey that it swallows. In this way it avoids drawing attention to itself while digesting its meal. It also has a unique joint between its head and neck that enables its jaws to open exceptionally wide in order to swallow larger prey.

DRAGONFISH (below) The stoplight loosejaw is a type of dragonfish. It has a pair of light organs that generates red light.

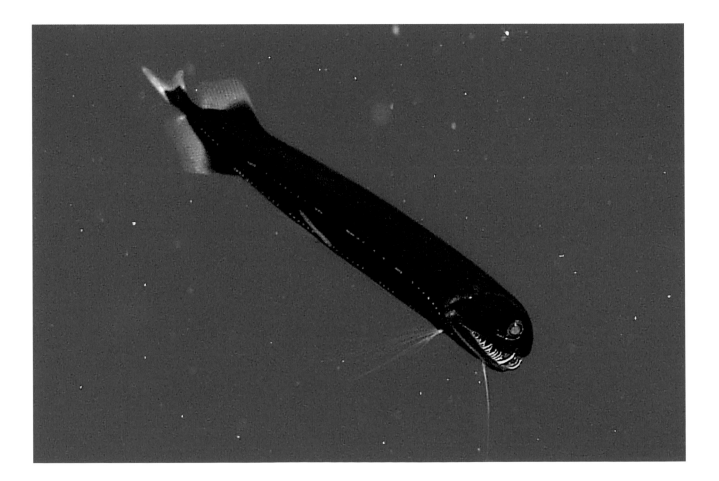

Into the Abyss

The abyssal realm extends from the lower limit of the midnight zone to the deep-sea floor, 6,000 metres below sea level. It is an extraordinary place of calm, far removed from storms at the surface. Its waters are between 0°C and 4°C, and the pressure is 400–600 times the atmospheric pressure at the surface.

The view from a submersible at these depths is often little more than marine snow. The steady trickle of particles from above takes the best part of a month to drift down and settle on the seabed. Sedimentation is slow, but a steady influx of clay, blown into the open ocean from the land, silt washed into the sea by rivers, and marine snow from the upper parts of the ocean blankets the topography so the sea floor appears flat and featureless, almost desert-like. This is the abyssal plain, the flattest place on Earth.

It is found at any depth between 3,000 metres and 6,000 metres, usually sandwiched between a mid-ocean ridge on one side and the foot of the continental slope on the other, and although the abyssal plain covers a

ANCIENT ECHINODERM (below)
The great West Indian sea lily is a species of stalked crinoid, a group of animals that has its origins about 485 million years ago.

large part of the surface of our planet, it is one of the least studied habitats on Earth.

The plain is less densely populated than elsewhere in the deep sea, but there is still a great diversity of animal life. Just above the sea floor, stalked sea lilies trap floating food particles, grenadier fish scan the sediments for the smell of food, and tripod fish park themselves on the seabed with elongated fins, their heads facing into the current. Sea stars creep about on hundreds of tube feet, consuming anything living or dead, brittle stars move on their flexible arms, scooping up organic remains, sea cucumbers plough the seabed, while polychaete worms, heart urchins and bivalve molluscs burrow directly into sediment, and the sea toad (actually a fish) walks across the seafloor with modified fins that look more like legs.

Many of these animals are able to live without food for many weeks, months or even years. Waiting is the norm here. Most organisms are ultimately dependent on whatever sinks down from above, but they can survive on these relatively meagre rations because, like the Antarctic, it

SEA TOAD (above) Sea toads are bottom-dwellers. They rest and 'walk' across the seabed on their stubby leg-like pectoral and pelvic fins, but can swim like any other fish, if they have a mind to.

is exceedingly cold and their metabolism is slow. Animals try to minimise their energy needs. They move very slowly or just hang about, waiting for something to turn up. Sometimes it doesn't.

Overfishing at the surface must have curtailed what some of these abyssal plain animals receive. Fish that once provided them with dead bodies and faecal matter have been hoisted out of the sea wholesale. Populations have plummeted and deep-sea creatures have been robbed of part of their basic foodstuff. Communities directly below major fishing grounds must have had a hard time, something scientists had not realised before now. Humans are not only depleting fish stocks, but the knock-on effect is to cause unknown damage to ecosystems on the deep sea floor.

Even so, under normal circumstances a bright, warm summer can boost productivity. Occasionally, huge pulses of organic material sink down after organisms such as diatoms bloom at the surface. They trigger a population explosion of mid-water creatures, such as salps, which feed on the algae, and when they die, their bodies not only add to the bonanza down below but also carry carbon to the seafloor, another climate change ally. These sudden pulses, however, can provide as much food in a few weeks as would normally arrive in several years. Imagine, then, the activity when a dead sperm whale lands on the doorstep.

TRACHYMEDUSAE (below)
This deep-sea relative of the Portuguese man o' war is living at a depth of 4,850 metres on the Porcupine Abyssal Plain, adjacent to Ireland's continental shelf in the northeast Atlantic.

Whalefall

The moment the carcass touches down, the intense pressure squeezes blood and oils from its body, and the enticing odours waft across the bottom of the sea. Every chemical sensor downstream is triggered and its owner on high alert and on the move. The ravening hordes painstakingly follow the smell back to its source. The feast has begun.

After just 25 minutes, the first of the dinner guests arrives, and it is a real bruiser – a female bluntnose six-gill shark. At 4–5 metres long, she is one of the world's largest and most powerful sharks, and, like most large animals down here, she glides languidly into view. She's not in any hurry. She takes a gigantic bite. Stiletto-like teeth in her top jaw give her purchase and comb-shaped teeth in the lower jaw do the slicing. She moves her head violently from side to side, sawing through flesh and sinew, her large green eyes drawn back into their sockets for protection, an automatic reflex lest the dead whale should fight back. Every mouthful leaves a gaping scar, allowing more fluids to escape and drift downstream.

Her sole occupancy doesn't last long. Another, even larger shark has picked up the smell from a kilometre away. She's another six-gill, and she wants the whale for herself. This species is territorial, and being bigger than the rest places her at the head of the queue, but as she bullies the smaller shark, more arrive. She tries to see them off with bites to their bodies and she rams them in their gills, their most sensitive part, but the prize is so attractive that incoming sharks overwhelm the large female and ramp up the action.

FOOD BONANZA (below)
1 The mutilated body of a sperm whale settles on the deep-sea floor.

2 A spider crab snacks on whale entrails, as a large six-gill shark glides past.

3 A feeding frenzy of bluntnose sixgill sharks on the floor of the Atlantic Ocean.

4 With the sharks gone, what remains of the whale carcass is taken over by spider crabs, deep-sea fish, hagfish, amphipods and any other creature that chances by.

1

2

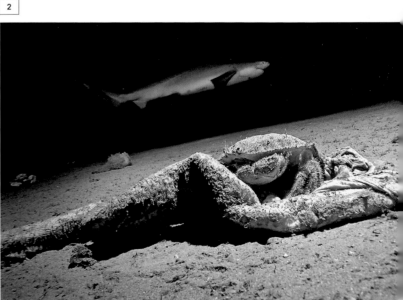

Watching events unfold from a deep-sea submersible was assistant producer Will Ridgeon. 'As we approached the carcass, we could see an enormous cloud of silt and sediment, and could just about make out the massive shapes of several six-gill sharks. At one point, there were seven huge females ripping into the whale, the largest not far off the length of the submersible. They were taking large chunks of blubber, but were also biting each other, and it was rather daunting when they turned on the submersible, with a 5-metre-long shark bumping the dome of the sub.'

Scary though it was, the frantic free-for-all was the first time anybody has witnessed such a shark feeding frenzy 800 metres down on the floor of the deep Atlantic Ocean.

With every bite, the sharks spill more scraps and smells into the current, and vibrations from the commotion travel across the seafloor to be picked up by some very sensitive legs. They belong to deep-sea spider crabs. They're slow and mechanical in their movements, and curiously they grip pieces of sponge with their back legs and hold it over their bodies. The function is unknown.

The crabs seem more reticent to join in. A large six-gill could slice one in half, and sometimes will. The crabs bide their time, shredding pieces of wayward entrails, but, three days after the whalefall, the sharks have had their fill and move on.

On the whale carcass, now barely recognisable but which still has plenty of leftovers, the spider crabs finally move in and are joined by deep-

3

4

sea shrimps, squat lobsters, dense swarms of small amphipods, and a procession of deep-sea fish. It has become the focus of an entire ecosystem, representing a massive input of food in a place where it is generally hard to come by. A single whalefall can provide as much organic material as a thousand years of marine snow. It is also a magnet for the non-scavengers, wily predators with a nose for a quick meal.

About a month after the sharks have departed, a shoal of silver scabbard fish appear. Their interest is not the whale meat or blubber, but the deep-sea foodies. These hunters are ribbon-shaped, over a metre long, and they have a shiny sheen like polished metal. They hang vertically, heads facing upwards, almost motionless in the water, where they are effectively invisible, but when they attack they are exceedingly fast. Using stealth, speed and their needle-sharp teeth, they grab the smaller fish and crustaceans milling about the dwindling banquet. For them, too, the whale has delivered a welcome bonanza, and when the whalebones have been picked clean and many of the animals have left, the story does not end. The skeleton itself lures in some unexpected and rather bizarre creatures.

Flowering snot worms, as they are known affectionately, or zombie worms, to be more tasteful, actually bore into the bones. At just 2–7 centimetres long, these little characters look more like plants than animals. They have red flower-like gills at one end, which gather oxygen from the water, and root-like structures at the other, which produce an acid that eats into the bone. In this way, they are firmly anchored and ready to digest the skeleton. They have no mouth or digestive tract, but their roots harbour symbiotic bacteria that help break down the fats and proteins and release the nutrients. How the worm absorbs them is unknown.

Another mystery has been a gender puzzle. When these creatures were first discovered in 2002, all the zombie worms examined by scientists proved to be female. There were no signs of males, until they dissected a worm and there inside the jelly-like tube that surrounds the worm were the males, up to 100 inside a single female.

Eventually, so many zombie worms bore into the carcass that it resembles a red shag-pile carpet, but many years after, when the whalebones are eventually digested completely, the adult worms die. However, their eggs and larvae live on. They float away on deep-sea currents and as long as they can find another carcass, the line will continue. These worms have been doing this for an awfully long time.

Thirty-million-year-old whale fossils have been found that show signs of having been digested by zombie worms. As long as there have been whales, there have been zombie worms, so they must have become specialised

'They were taking large chunks of blubber, but were also biting each other, and it was rather daunting when they turned on the submersible, with a 4.5-metre-long shark bumping the dome of the sub.' WILL RIDGEON, Assistant Producer

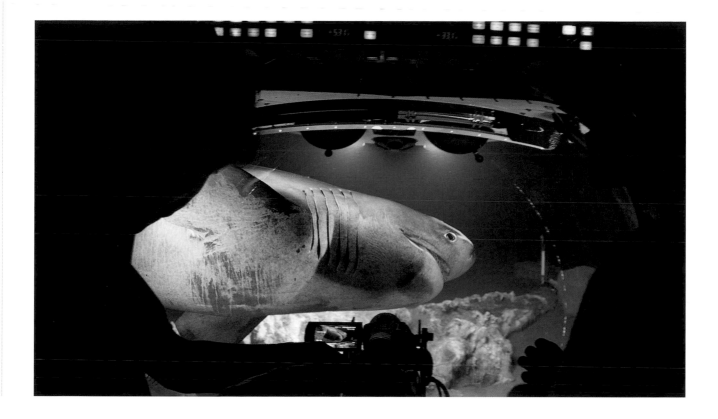

A BRUSH WITH DANGER

(above) The camera crew in the submersible has a close encounter with a 4.5-metre-long female six-gill shark. It swims close to the sub and bumps and mouths the acrylic dome.

bone-feeders before whales evolved. Lo and behold, the fossil skeletons of plesiosaurs and ancient sea turtles that lived about 100 million years ago have been found with the tell-tale excavations of zombie worms.

In modern seas, several species of zombie worms have been found on a range of whale skeletons in different parts of the ocean. Speculation among marine biologists is that below the extensive migration routes of the great whales, there are whale graveyards that act as stepping-stones. By hopping from one carcass to the next, this unique ecosystem of deep-sea creatures, including the enigmatic zombie worms, can spread throughout the oceans of the world.

But what happens if the whales are not sinking down? During the nineteenth and twentieth centuries intense whaling annihilated stocks of the giant whales, so their carcasses would not have reached the deep sea. After a time of plenty, when the old-style whalers moved in and discarded whale skeletons, more modern whaling techniques saw many of the stepping-stones removed and, when the whales were brought almost to the point of extinction, very few whales were sinking to the seabed at all. Like overfishing, what humans did at the surface must have had an impact on the animals at the bottom of the deep sea, and we are only now beginning to understand it.

Deepest of the Deeps

The deepest parts of the ocean are in the hadal zone. Here, ocean trenches plunge into the deepest parts of the ocean, the deepest being the Challenger Deep, 10,984 metres below the surface of the Pacific Ocean in the bottom of the Mariana Trench. It is a place of crushing pressures – a thousand times that at the surface – yet even here the ocean is gradually revealing its deepest secrets.

The walls of ocean trenches are lined with pure white sea anemones, like elaborate wallpaper. The floor is carpeted by mats of bacteria, and there are flattened sand castles inhabited by amoeba-like creatures – xenophyophores – whose filaments have many nuclei but no cell walls, making them amongst the largest single cells on Earth. They're 10 centimetres long!

Phallic-shaped spoonworms make star patterns in bottom sediments, and there are many types of sea cucumbers, including the aptly named sea pigs, which plough across the sea floor in small herds and have a striking resemblance to domestic pigs.

SEA PIG (below) Sea pigs are sea cucumbers with huge tube feet, resembling legs. They appear to snuffle about in the sediment like pigs, extracting food particles from sea floor deposits. They have a preference for freshly fallen food from the surface, which they detect by smell.

SNAILFISH (above) This species of snailfish is endemic to the Kermadec Trench in the southwest Pacific. It lives, along with deep-sea brittlestars, at a depth of 7,166 metres, making it one of the deepest living fish.

The amphipods are monsters. Most species in the deep sea are little more than 2–3 centimetres long, but these trench-living 'supergiants' are ten times bigger, up to 34 centimetres long, another example of deep-sea gigantism. For defence, they push up their spiny tails, like thorn bushes. Any inquisitive fish gets a stab in the nose.

Of the fishes, cusk eels and snailfish have been found in trenches, each trench with its own distinct species. The deepest fish observed in its natural environment is a new species at a depth of 8,145 metres in the Mariana Trench. This snailfish is pale pink, has a face uncannily like that of a cartoon dachshund, with ghostly wing-like pectoral fins and a body behind the head that waves about like wet tissue paper, as if it has no structure. Scientists have called it, appropriately, the 'ethereal snailfish'.

That fish can survive these pressures at extreme depths is amazing in itself, and they can do so because of special chemicals that stabilise proteins. Without them, the intense pressure would distort proteins in cells, but the process only works at pressures down to 8,400 metres; any deeper and a new biochemistry would be needed. It means these snailfish and cusk eels are living at the depth-limit that fish can survive, and that the bottom of the very deepest of the deeps is out of reach even for the fish.

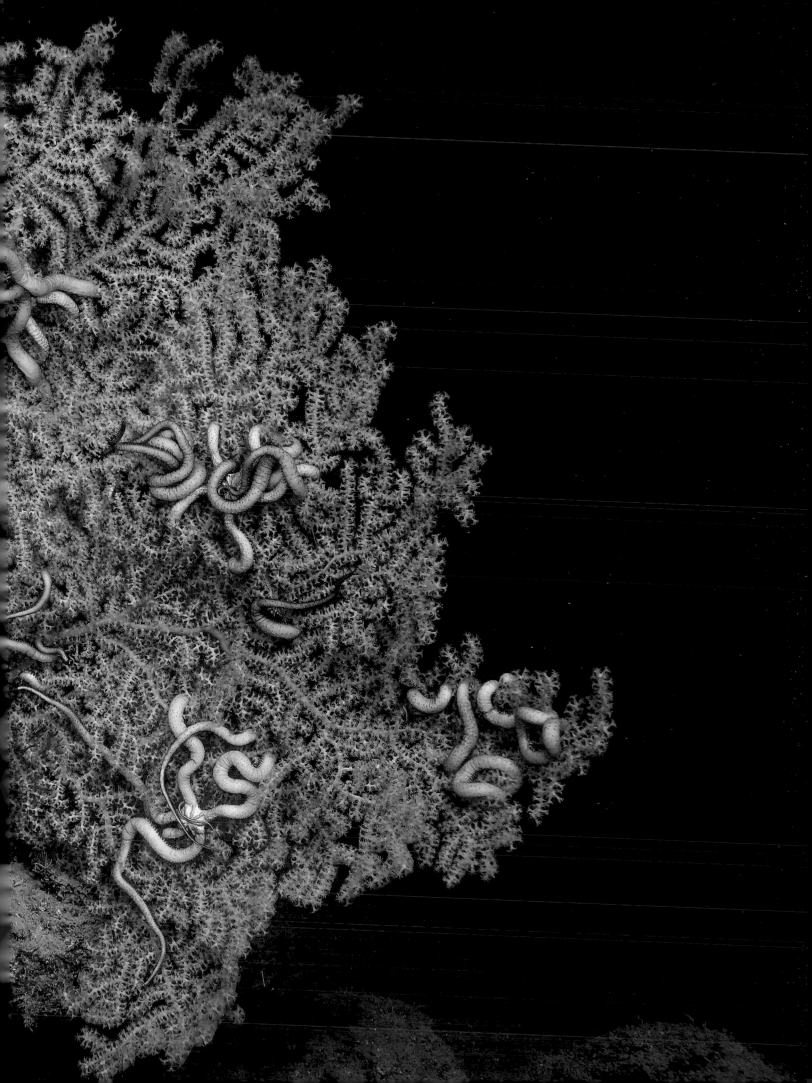

Hairy Crabs and Sea Snail Nurseries

The Mid-Ocean Ridge is one of the places where molten magma oozes out to form the tectonic plates that shift the continents about on our planet's surface. Most of the ridge is hidden under many hundreds of metres of water, and with all that heat energy close to the seabed there is an opportunity for marine life to move in and take advantage of it, but on very different terms than in the rest of the deep sea. The energy that underpins the whalefall's transient ecosystem or the deep-sea coral reef's animal community must come originally from all those photosynthesising

SHAGGY CRAB (below and opposite) The deep-sea yeti crab lives close to cold methane seeps and grows its own food. It has bacteria gardens on its claws, which it waves rhythmically in the seep water in a comical dance.

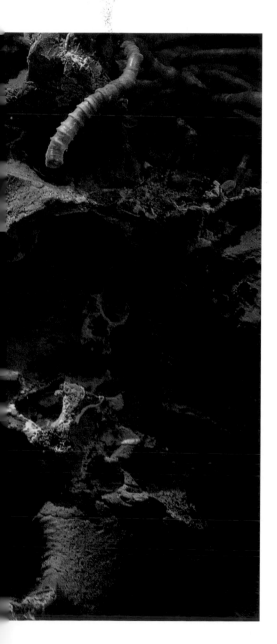

phytoplankton at the surface, but there are other systems at the bottom of the ocean that do not rely on the Sun at all.

In some parts of the deep sea floor, methane (natural gas) and hydrogen sulphide (bad eggs smell) leak from fissures in rocks warmed by heat emanating from deep within the Earth. Where the discharge is at the same temperature or slightly warmer than the surrounding seawater it is known generally as a cold seep. If the water is hot it is called a hydrothermal vent. Both features have their own special animal communities.

The drivers of both of these ecosystems are bacteria and other kinds of primitive microbes. They process the methane or hydrogen sulphide to make sugars. In this way, they derive their energy from chemical processes, rather than from the Sun like plants and photosynthetic bacteria do, and so are known as chemosynthetic bacteria. They, in turn, are food or provide food for the other members of the seep and vent communities.

Many creatures are attracted to cold seeps. King crabs feed on the white or orange mats of bacteria which thrive on the chemicals spewed out around the seep, and large tubeworms have symbiotic bacteria embedded in their tissues to supply them with nutrients, but one of the oddest creatures must be a little squat lobster. It was found at a cold seep off the coast of Costa Rica and its rather hairy appearance gained it the nickname of 'yeti crab'. There are several species around the world, but this one's body and especially its claws are covered with bristles in which it 'farms' bacteria. In a bizarre dance, it waves them over the active seep, thus maximising the bacteria's exposure to the chemicals in the discharge. To feed, it draws the bristles across its comb-like mouthparts and swallows the bolus of bacteria.

'It was strange and a little unnerving to be working a thousand metres down at the bottom of the sea, but you quickly focus on the filming and it becomes business as usual.' WILL RIDGEON, Assistant Producer

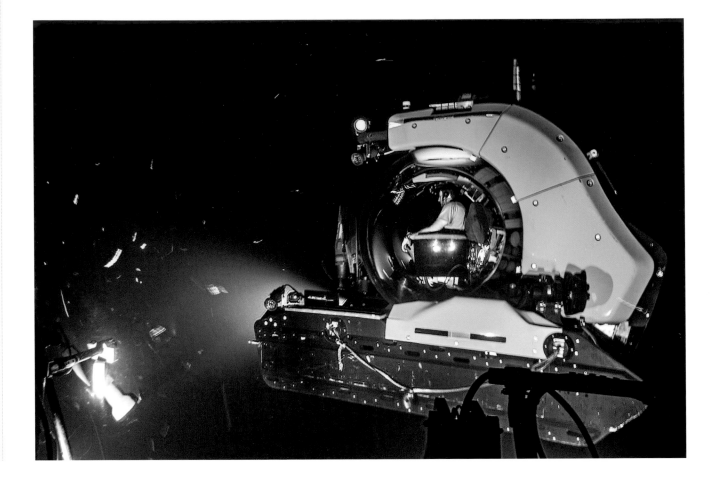

Will Ridgeon went in search of them. His submersible had to drift down to the seabed, about 1,000 metres below the surface. His task was to film the crabs' unusual behaviour, but first he had to find them.

'It took over an hour to reach the seabed, which was a featureless desert of mud, so finding the small groups of yeti crabs in the pitch black was a real challenge. However, after flying for some time over empty mud, it was an impressive sight to come across the large rock hydrate mounds covered with brilliant white yeti crabs. They wave their hairy arms back and forth, almost in unison. You could see why they have also been nicknamed "dancing crabs".

'It was strange and a little unnerving to be working a thousand metres down at the bottom of the sea, but you quickly focus on the filming and it becomes business as usual. We saw how the crabs seemed to jostle for the best positions, probably to occupy the best spots to farm bacteria. Then they would settle down and wave their arms.

'One of the unusual things we observed were deep-sea shrimps that crept closer and closer to the crabs, before zipping in and stealing a

YETI CRAB COUNTRY (below) *Deep Rover* approaches the cold seep area where yeti crabs are to be found at a depth of about 1,000 metres, off the coast of Costa Rica.

PILOT'S EYE VIEW (above) The view from the acrylic dome of the submersible as it approaches the cold seep area.

mouthful of food from the crab's hairy arms. We did feel sorry for the crabs, patiently cultivating their crop only to have the shrimps steal it.'

The yeti crab is a wonderful example of the way the deep sea is surprising us. It seems that every time that deep-sea biologists dip a toe in the water they chance upon something new and strange, and a visit to a cold seep field on the Southern Hydrate Ridge, to the west of Oregon, was no exception. The seep itself is known as Einstein's Grotto, a site of vigorous venting of methane along with extensive white mats of bacteria, but it has some curious neighbours. Scientists call the adjacent site 'Neptunea's Nursery', *Neptunea* being a genus of gastropod mollusc related to the common whelk. The nursery is a scattering of vertical yellow cylinders, each set on the top of a rounded cobble. From a submersible, it looks like an aerial view of a desert city with sallow skyscrapers. The towers are stacks of the mollusc's yellow eggs glued together, and some are seen with the mother snail perched on top babysitting her offspring, but they take more than a year to develop and hatch out, so the mothers are often dead before their babies emerge, their empty shells quickly occupied by deep-sea hermit crabs.

Mud Volcanoes

The Southern Hydrate Ridge gets its name from the way methane may not always be in a gaseous state. At the high pressures and low temperatures at the bottom of the ocean, methane can occur in its solid state, known as a gas hydrate. It forms solid ice within the sea floor. From time to time the methane changes back, triggering mud volcanoes, and producer Orla Doherty wanted to be there when it happened.

'We were a few days into our shoot in the Gulf of Mexico, when Dr Mandy Joye, who was guiding our dives in the submersibles, whispered in my ear that bubbles had been seen at another site. We decided to risk it and, when we reached the right coordinates, the ship's sonar picked up a plume of bubbles about 600 metres below us. However, once we were down, there was no sign of them. We combed the seabed for an hour and then just ahead of us we saw a large bubble, about the size of a basketball, rise into the water column, trailing bottom sediment behind, like the tail of a space rocket. More followed, and very quickly giant bubbles of methane surrounded us, erupting from what had been a flat abyssal plain. It was as if we'd voyaged to another planet.

'We returned to the site twice more, but each time there was barely a puff coming out. We had been lucky on the first visit, and Mandy had never seen the site so active. The deep had given up one of its great secret events, but only the once.'

GAS ERUPTION (below) Bubbles of methane rise in the water column, each one leaving a trail of sediment behind like a rocket trail.

Pools of Despair

In the same part of the Gulf of Mexico, the mud volcanoes expose ancient deposits of salt that have been buried since Jurassic times. The salt mixes with the water, and very dense brine, eight times saltier than normal seawater, accumulates in the hollow. It looks uncannily like a mystical pool as calm as a millpond at the bottom of the sea. It has a clear 'shoreline' separating the water of different densities, and over time living organisms have formed a 'beach'.

Cold seep mussels are common along the edge of the brine pool. They have their food manufactured for them by symbiotic bacteria living in their tissues, which utilise methane seeping from the seabed. The mussels create the shore where deep-sea eels lever themselves into open mussel shells and extract their contents, and crabs and squat lobsters hunt or scavenge amongst the debris. The brine itself is a death trap. Some fish seem to know the danger, while others blunder in and, if they enter accidentally,

BRINE POOL (below) The 'shoreline' of cold seep mussels demarcates the hypersaline brine pool (right) from the rest of the ocean (left). A fish is careful not to enter the pool while hunting amongst the shellfish.

' Trying to manoeuvre the mini camera on the end of a robotic arm
took a lot of skill from the submersible pilots, and they captured
some extraordinary footage. **'**   WILL RIDGEON, Assistant Producer

NOT MAKING WAVES (above) The
submersible manoeuvres carefully to
within a few centimetres of the brine
pool. The brine is so dense that the
craft could 'land' on its surface.

they die a slow, squirming death. Their dead bodies can remain submerged
there for years.

'Sitting on the shore of the pool,' remembers Will Ridgeon, 'watching
the brine lapping up against the mussels, it was easy to forget that you were
600 metres underwater. It was a real contrast: the mussel-bed shoreline
was teeming with life, while the toxic black pool was littered with dead
and dying animals. You could see fish and squid swimming out across the
deadly brine, but few seemed to make it across alive.

'Trying to manoeuvre the mini camera on the end of a robotic arm
took a lot of skill from the submersible pilots, and they captured some
extraordinary footage. It gave a unique view of the extraordinary number of
creatures living amongst the mussels around the shore.'

Scientists have called such a pool the 'Jacuzzi of Despair'. And, if
brine pools seem like a hell on Earth, there are even more hostile places
down here.

Super-Hot Vents

In geologically active regions on the margins of the Earth's tectonic plates, the cracks in seabed rocks spew out not cool water but superhot water at temperatures in excess of 400°C. These underwater geysers are the hydrothermal vents. Cracks and crevasses in the rock allow cold seawater to seep towards the Earth's fiery interior, where it heats to very high temperatures and accumulates a heavy load of minerals. As the superhot water hits the cold seawater, the minerals precipitate out, building huge chimneys up to 40 metres tall, the height of a 12-storey building. They gush plumes of black or white 'smoke', scenes reminiscent of the chimneys of the Industrial Revolution. The black smokers have the highest temperatures and emit sulphur-based compounds, while white smokers are cooler and spew out barium, calcium and silicon. Both are home to bacteria that feed on the chemicals they emit, and they, in turn, succour more communities of strange deep-sea animals.

Each vent has its own assemblage. Giant tubeworms, giant mussels and clams, squat lobsters, eel-shaped fish, amphipods, scale-worms, sea anemones and small sea snails live directly next to the vents, and visitors might include octopuses with fins resembling flapping ears, earning them the nickname 'Dumbo octopuses'.

BLIND SHRIMPS (below) Young shrimps have eyes and live in the twilight zone where they feed on marine snow, which is derived from photosynthetic organisms. Later they migrate to black smoker vents, lose their eyes and feed on chemosynthetic organisms.

DUMBO OCTOPUS (above) These deep-sea octopuses can be found at all depths down to 7,000 metres, the deepest of any octopus. Most are about 20–30 centimetres long, although one species is 1.8 metres long. They visit deep-sea vents and pick off the residents.

At vents on the Mid-Ocean Ridge, there are swarms of an especially interesting shrimp. The little vivid-orange crustacean has no eyes, but appears to have a sensor on its back that probably detects light from the vent. The source of the mainly near-infrared light is not entirely clear, but it is important to the shrimp because the little creature has a strange way of farming its life-giving bacteria. It harbours a population in its mouth and under modified gill covers. To feed them with minerals, the shrimp must position itself directly on the border between the cold, oxygenated ocean water and the hot, mineral-rich vent water. If it drifts into the hot water and stays a moment too long it cooks, and if it is too far from the vent its bacteria die.

Origins of Life

The extreme conditions in and around these vent sites are hostile to most other life forms on Earth, but could they be the kinds of places where alien life might arise? Is it too far-fetched to consider that hydrothermal vents at the bottom of oceans on geologically active planets or moons, such as Jupiter's moons Europa and Ganymede (which has more surface water than the Earth and is ten times as deep) and Saturn's Enceladus, are places where life could start? Europa is very cold and covered by ice, but underneath the ice it is thought to have a warm, salty ocean, and huge geysers have been seen venting water vapour up to 160 kilometres above the surface, so the moon appears to be active. Enceladus is warmer than expected just a few metres below its icy surface, and could have a liquid ocean just a few kilometres beneath. Might there be life under the ice? One discovery on Earth demonstrates how it might have started.

At the Lost City Vent Field in the mid-Atlantic, the vents are cooler and alkaline, very different from the acidic black smokers. The thirty or so chimneys are up to 60 metres high, taller than the leaning Tower of Pisa, and made of calcium carbonate (chalk). The water gushing out is a relatively cool 40–90°C, and it releases methane and hydrogen into the water, but no hydrogen sulphide.

The vent community reflects the calcium content of the water – gastropod and bivalve molluscs with calcium shells, polychaete worms, amphipods and ostracods, along with primitive microbes that exist in biofilms inside the vents. It has led scientists to consider whether such vents could be the birthplace of life, a place where the vent environment generated chemicals that were the starting point for more complex organic molecules and where chemosynthetic organisms created energy cycles that enabled life to evolve. It seems like the ideal home for the genesis of life on Earth, and maybe even elsewhere in the universe.

Of all the ocean realms, exploration of the deep sea is pushing the boundaries of science and technology. Almost every time a submersible or a drop-camera enters the deep-sea environment, it comes back with something new. It has left normally hard-nosed scientists lost for words. They have found mounds of 'strange little spheres', 'feathery wispy things' and 'green stringy things', as well as jelly-like blobs that could only be classified as 'animals' but little else. All these creatures were totally unknown, not only new species, but also entirely new forms of life. The deep sea really is throwing up the biggest surprises of all.

LOST CITY (opposite) These spires are made from freshly deposited calcium carbonate. As it ages, it becomes as hard as concrete, so the towers and spires can be nearly 60 metres tall.

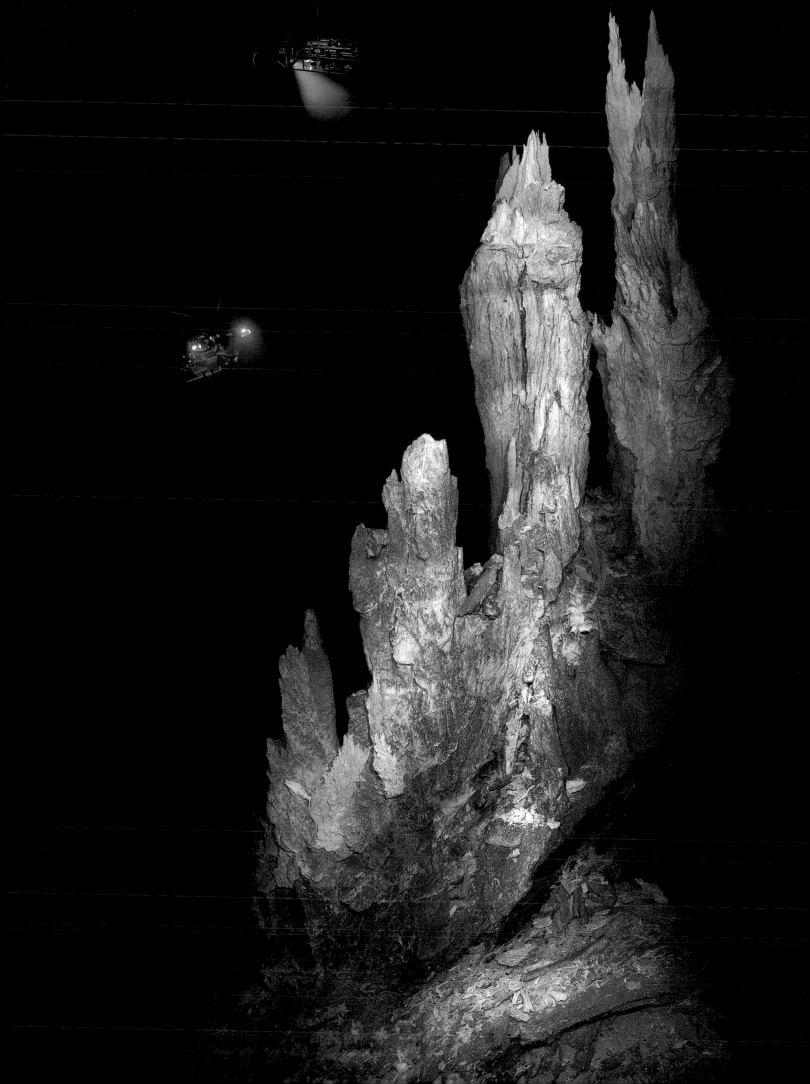

chapter seven

Our Ocean

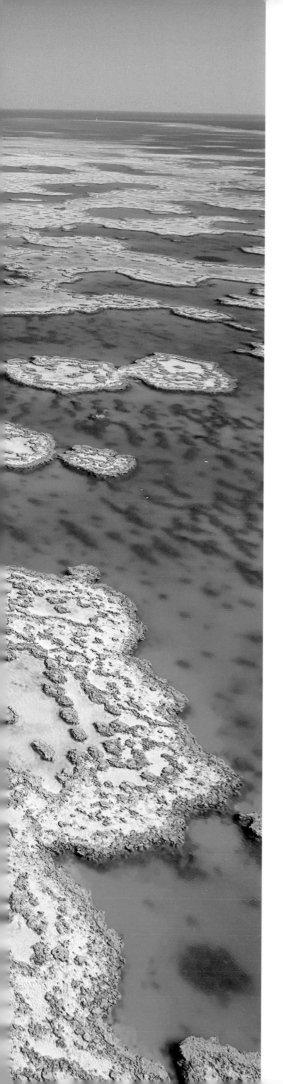

CORAL ATOLL (left) Tidal channels, which cut through the coral reef, fill and drain the central lagoon on Aldabra in the Seychelles, the second largest coral atoll (after Kiritimati) in the world.

STORMY SEAS (previous page) A small shoal of bigeyed scad swims beneath the breakers in the Sea of Cortez (Gulf of California).

During the making of *Blue Planet II*, our production teams visited places where nobody had been before, encountered new species of marine life, and witnessed remarkable feats of ingenuity; but, aside from the sumptuous images, and the magic, wonder and surprise, no matter where in the world they went, they saw signs that all was not well with our oceans.

In the past, we believed that the seas were so vast and their wildlife so limitless that our actions would bear little consequence, but, sadly, we now know this is not true. The health of our oceans, and, therefore the entire planet, is under threat. The oceans are changing at a faster rate and in more ways than at any other time in our history. So great is the extent of the challenges they face, many believe our oceans have reached crisis point. The world is at a crossroads. Do something now and we could step back from the brink; do nothing, and we are in uncharted waters.

First the Good News… or is it?

Since the International Whaling Commission announced that there should be a 'pause' in commercial whaling from the 1985–1986 season, many populations of the great whales have been slowly recovering. Blue whales have returned to the their feeding grounds off California, substantial numbers of gray whales are undertaking their long journeys along the Pacific coast of North America, humpback super-groups have been spotted off South Africa (see p.14), great sperm whale gatherings occur off Sri Lanka (see p.226), and a hundred southern right whales (the 'right whales to catch') pitch up regularly at the Head of the Bight in Southern Australia. These are events that, until very recently, have been unheard of for a hundred years or more, but, although some whale populations have recovered, the ocean in which they live is deteriorating. Shane Gero, of the Dominica Sperm Whale Research Project (see p.188), is seeing at first hand what the consequences might be.

'In one way, sperm whales are doing better than a lot of other species. They're not really hunted any more, but here in the Caribbean, the population is in critical decline. The seventeen families that I've worked with during the past decade are all shrinking. Mortality is high, and it's probably because of people. They live in the most urban part of sperm whale habitat, right next to an island filled with people, so boats hit them, they get entangled in fishing gear, and they swim through run-off from the island. And, that's a big problem. One in three calves doesn't survive to its first birthday. If that carries on, all the families of the animals I've come to know as individuals will be gone before I retire. It's tragic. It's shocking, but probably avoidable. We need to make changes now.

'One of the worst things we have done to the oceans is ignore them. Below the surface, a lot has changed, particularly acoustically. In the whale's world, beneath the surface, sound is the most important thing, and we've been putting a lot of loud noise into the ocean. It's harder for sperm whales to talk to each other.'

And this doesn't only apply to whales. The tropical coral reef is a naturally noisy place (see p.106), and we are only just realising how important sound is to the animals living there. Studying them has been Steve Simpson, of the University of Exeter. He has designed a piece of underwater kit with four directional hydrophones that records the sounds and enables him to work out where they are coming from.

'Listening in surround sound, we can work out who's making which noises and why. Are they trying to impress each other or to scare something

OCEAN GIANT (opposite) A blue whale surfaces in the Sea of Cortez (Gulf of California).

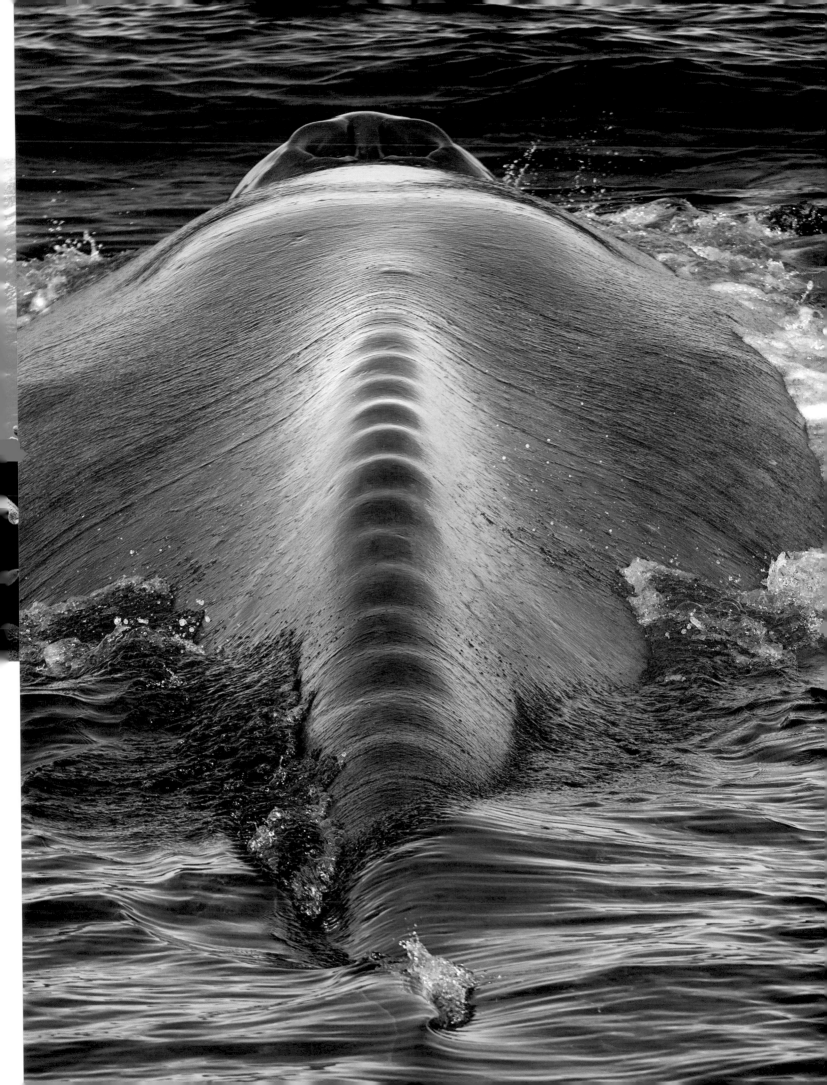

Out of Sight, Out of Mind

Noise is a form of pollution, although more usually, perhaps, we think of pollution as noxious chemicals spewed into the environment from industry and agriculture, or untreated sewage from homes poured directly into the sea. It was something that we became aware of in the 1960s, our attention drawn particularly to the pesticide DDT by concerned scientists such as Rachel Carson in books like *Silent Spring*. We were alerted to the insidious nature of pollutants, the way persistent chemicals build in the food chain and eventually poison apex predators, including us. In some parts of the world, particularly the Arctic, the build-up of dangerous chemicals has been so great that some affected marine creatures, such as polar bears and beluga whales, could be legitimately labelled 'hazardous waste'. The problem, however, far from going away, is as persistent as the chemicals themselves.

Centuries ago, when our forebears first poured pollutants into the sea, either deliberately or accidentally, the naive thinking was that they were out of sight and out of mind. Today, though, some of them are coming back

HEALTH SCARE (below) A small pod of bottlenose dolphins surfaces off the coast of Florida. Many young dolphins here have been lost due to mercury poisoning.

to haunt us. Chemicals banned during the 1970s, for example, are to be found in the bodies of amphipods brought up from the deepest parts of the sea, the Mariana and Kermadec trenches. Scientists from the University of Newcastle analysed the amphipods' fatty tissues, and they were found to contain toxic chemicals, such as polychlorinated biphenyls (PCBs) and polybrominated diphenyl esters (PBDEs), at unexpectedly high levels. Concentrations were about the same as in the tissues of crustaceans from Suruga Bay, one of the most polluted bays in Japan.

PCBs were widely used in electrical insulators and PBDEs are used to reduce the flammability of furniture and furnishings, and they must have found their way into the sea as effluents, leaks from landfill sites or through industrial accidents. A recent study by scientists from Canada, Alaska, Denmark and Norway has shown that polar bears, especially in East Greenland and Svalbard, are contaminated with PBDEs, causing females to develop both female and male sex organs. It also showed how these chemicals build in the food chain. One compound was seventy-one times more concentrated in the bears than in the seals on which they mainly feed.

In 2016, exceptionally high levels of PCBs were found in a member of the UK's last resident killer whale pods. The female, known to whale watchers as Lulu, was washed ashore on the Isle of Tiree, off the west coast of Scotland. She had PCB levels more than thirty times the limit above which damage to health is known. In a BBC News interview, Dr Andrew Brownlow, a veterinary pathologist at Scotland's Rural College, described her as 'one of the most contaminated individuals that we've ever looked at'. The examination revealed that the PCBs had caused Lulu to be infertile, and, as the other animals in the pod are likely to have similar levels of the chemical in their tissues, the probability is that the group will eventually die out.

Mercury is another hazard. Off the Florida Keys and in Everglades coastal waters, an international team of scientists working with Florida International University has found that bottlenose dolphins there have exceptionally high levels of mercury in their tissues, the highest ever recorded. This has an impact on their immune systems, making them more vulnerable to diseases. Mangroves are a source of that mercury. They transform mercury to its toxic form – methyl mercury – and this is washed out by the tides into coastal waters, where it is picked up and concentrated at each step in the food chain. Thus, the mercury is consumed far from the coal-burning plants that were its original source.

Global Litter

In January 2017, a 6-metre-long Cuvier's beaked whale continually beached itself on the island of Sotra, near Bergen, in Norway. It was so ill that, after several failed attempts to guide it back out to sea, veterinarians were forced to euthanise the weak and emaciated animal. When they came to do a post-mortem examination, they were in for a shock. Its stomach was filled with about thirty large plastic bags, together with smaller bags that once contained bread, chocolate bar wrappers, and other human litter. The animal, according to scientists, must have been in considerable pain for a long time, its gut blocked by the plastic and other refuse. It had probably mistaken the bags for squid, on which it normally feeds. It was a grisly reminder that the oceans and all that lives in them are facing a new threat from humankind – death by litter, especially plastic.

It has often been said that litter is a curse of the modern age. Much of the debris from our 'throw-away society' ends up in landfill sites, but not all. Millions of tonnes end up in the sea, and in some parts of the ocean, such as off the coast of South Korea, there are 10 billion pieces of litter per square kilometre of sea. Inevitably, this has an impact on marine life.

The online data portal LITTERBASE has taken data from 1,267 scientific papers from 1960 to 2017 and found that 1,286 marine species (and counting), especially seabirds, fish, crustaceans and mammals, interact with litter in the ocean. Of those affected, about 34 per cent of

PLASTIC LOAD (above) Some of the plastic bags found in the stomach of a Cuvier's beaked whale.

THE VICTIM (below) The Cuvier's beaked whale was euthanised.

animals eat it, 31 per cent live in or on it or hide under it, and 30 per cent are trapped or become entangled by it. They also revealed that close to 70 per cent of all the litter in the ocean is plastic.

Plastic is found in all the world's oceans. Ocean currents and surface winds move it about the globe. Denser pieces sink to the seabed, while downwellings pull less dense pieces into the abyss. Floating plastic concentrates in ocean gyres (see p.214) or piles up in enclosed bays, gulfs and seas. Some is thrown up on beaches, including those in some of the world's most out of the way places.

The remotest beaches must be on uninhabited Henderson Island, one of the Pitcairn group of islands in the South Pacific. It is 5,000 kilometres from the nearest major landmass, so it should be one of the few places on Earth where humans have had little impact. Researchers from the University of Tasmania, however, have found that 98.9 per cent of the debris dumped by the sea onto the island's beaches was not natural materials, such as palm fronds and driftwood, but plastic. Up to 672 pieces per square metre were on the surface of the beach and up to 4,497 pieces per square metre were buried to a depth of 10 centimetres under the sand. The scientists estimated that 37.7 million pieces of plastic, weighing about 17.6 tonnes, has been washed up on the island.

These plastic objects can be mistaken by wildlife for food, causing enormous suffering. Plastic bags and the larger pieces of plastic block the intestines of whales, sea turtles and birds, such as albatrosses, or kill chicks because their parents have fed them plastics. Lucy Quinn has been monitoring the albatross chicks on Bird Island, a remote island in the South Georgia archipelago (see p.223).

'We follow the chicks from when they are first laid as an egg, right through to when they fledge, and for a wandering albatross this can take a year. The birds have been ringed here on Bird Island since the 1950s, so we've been able to follow individuals for their entire life.'

Wandering albatrosses spend much of their life soaring across the ocean, so they are not easy to study. However, what they feed to their chicks is an indication of what they are finding during their time away from the nest.

'Albatrosses have the ability to regurgitate the bits of food that they cannot digest, and from that we can work out what they've been eating. A healthy chick should have in its diet food such as squid and fish, so we can find squid beaks and fish bones in whatever they cough up, but from last season, the birds regurgitated bottle caps, wrapping, plastic gloves, and large pieces of plastic, and one bird brought up an intact light bulb!'

Plastic Soup

Plastic is usually broken down by ultraviolet light from the sun and wave action into smaller particles, with 92 per cent of plastic in the ocean less than the size of a grain of rice. This is entering the food chain at its lowest level. At the Plymouth Marine Laboratory, scientists have videoed zooplankton ingesting not their more usual food of phytoplankton, but minute pieces of plastic. It was thought that these tiny animals could distinguish between different types of algae and suchlike in the phytoplankton, but, if the plastic particles are of a similar size, they are mistaking them for food. In some cases, the plastic is egested within hours. In others, it is retained for several days, where it blocks the gut and the little creatures are unable to feed properly – the same problem as with the Norwegian whale, only in miniature.

Another type of microplastic includes small particles abraded from car tyres when driving, and fibres from synthetic textiles when washing them. About 2 per cent are microbeads from cosmetics. All told, these microplastics account for about a third of the around 8 million tonnes of plastic released into the oceans each year, and they make up 85 per cent of human-made debris washed up on shores all around the world.

RUBBISH DUMP (above) Laysan albatrosses are surrounded by plastic and other debris washed ashore by a tsunami at Midway Atoll National Wildlife Reserve.

Microfibres from a synthetic fleece jacket, for example, are lost at a rate of 1.7 grams per wash or about 4,500 fibres per gram of clothing per wash, with older jackets losing twice as many fibres as new ones. About 40 per cent of fibres pass through sewage treatment plants and then on to the ocean, where they do not biodegrade like natural fibres.

The small size of synthetic fibres means they are readily eaten by marine life and, like many pollutants, are concentrated in the food chain. Animals that have eaten microfibres have been shown to eat less food and, over time, their growth is stunted. The fibres also introduce toxins into the food chain. They bind with harmful chemical pollutants in wastewater, such as pesticides and those dangerous PCBs and flame-retardants, and the fibres themselves are often coated with chemicals to make them water-repellent. The poisons are then concentrated in animal tissues. Whether eating seafood contaminated with plastic microfibres is dangerous to humans is as yet unknown, but there is no getting away from it: we are at the top of the food chain, and we catch the fish and shellfish that eat the zooplankton that eat the fibres.

A study of seafood from Indonesia and California by scientists from the University of California, Davis, and Hasanuddin University, Indonesia, found that plastic particles, rather than microfibres, were the overriding contaminants in 28 per cent of fish caught in Indonesia, but plastic microfibres dominated in 25 per cent of fish in California. The discrepancy is thought to be down to the fact that washing machines are less prevalent in Indonesia, and high performance fabrics, such as fleeces, are not so common there. However, one thing the authors of the report in the journal *Nature* highlight is that this is the first time these fibres have been found in fish sold for human consumption, raising more concerns regarding human health.

A hint of what could happen to us comes from a study of bottlenose dolphins off the coast of Sarasota. Here, there is high mortality in first-born calves. Speculation is that their mother's milk is contaminated by microplastics, along with any toxic chemicals that attach to the plastic, such as PCBs. The microplastics are in the fish consumed by the mother dolphins, and these are the same kind of fish that we eat.

To top it all, geologists at Kamilo Beach on Big Island, Hawaii, have found an unusual type of rock. It is made from fragments of volcanic rock, beach sand, seashells, coral... and plastic! It probably formed when the plastic was melted by fire, say, from a barbecue on the beach or from hot volcanic lava, and it glued together all the other natural materials. They have called it 'plastiglomerate', and, if such newly made rock remains intact for any length of time and is buried at the bottom of the sea, it will leave in the geological record a marker that says 'humans were here' – the first rocks of the Anthropocene, the proposed name for a geological epoch that covers the period that humanity has had a significant impact on the Earth.

NEW ROCK (below) A piece of 'plastiglomerate' found on a beach in Hawaii.

Rise of the Jellies

One of the first environmental issues to face people who work on the ocean was overfishing. Today, over 30 per cent of global fish stocks are thought to be fished at a biologically unsustainable level, but just after the end of the Second World War nobody was concerned. The fish markets were full, and catches kept coming.

An early wake-up call was the collapse of the cod fishery on the Grand Banks in the northwest Atlantic, and the declaration of a moratorium in 1992. For 500 years, fishing communities in Newfoundland, on the east coast of Canada, depended on cod, and they fished it sustainably, but in the 1950s new catch technology gave rise to heavy exploitation and a partial collapse of cod stocks in the 1970s. By the 1990s, there were few fish to catch. Thirty-five thousand fishermen and fish processing workers from more than 400 coastal communities were immediately out of work, although fishing was not over entirely.

With cod removed from the food chain, other creatures proliferated, especially snow crab and northern shrimp, and nowadays the fishery for these invertebrates, in economic terms, matches the cod fishery it replaced. However, as long as shrimp fishing goes on, the cod are unlikely to return in significant numbers, because most juvenile cod are caught long before they grow to commercial sizes by the fine mesh trawls needed to catch the shrimp. The problem is self-perpetuating.

In some parts of the world, overfishing has created other, even less welcome ecological changes. There's a jellyfish boom. There can be so many that they threaten any surviving fish stocks. They compete for food, devour fish eggs and larvae, and kill adult fish, and they can survive in low-oxygen environments where fish cannot. They clog the cooling water intakes of coastal power stations, they devastate saltwater fish farms, and they cause tourist bathing beaches to close.

Along the Namibian coast, over-harvested fish stocks have resulted in jellyfish accounting for considerably more biomass than do fish. Off the coast of Japan, monster Nomura's jellyfish, with bells up to two metres across, have been concentrated in such numbers that, on one occasion, a large fishing trawler snagged a swarm in its net, tried to haul it aboard, and capsized, the crew rescued by other fishing boats. Invertebrates, it seems, are in the ascendancy, and not only jellies.

Populations of octopus, squid and cuttlefish have increased too; at least, scientists think they have. In the vastness of the ocean, estimates are notoriously difficult to get right because they depend on the number of

GIANT JELLIES (above) A huge swarm of giant Nomura's jellyfish have been caught in fishing nets off the coast of Japan.

cephalopods caught, and catch sizes do not necessarily reflect the size of the population. This was one of the factors behind the overfishing of cod and herring – poor statistics. At the University of Adelaide, however, marine biologists have looked at catch statistics from 32 scientific surveys and countless fisheries records, including those difficult to obtain, to compile 60 years' worth of reliable data, and they can see a trend.

Cephalopod populations have boomed since the 1950s. The reason is harder to pin down, but the timescale is longer than normal ocean cycles, so there is more than a hint that humans have been involved. Catching the fish that eat squid and octopuses or compete with them for food creates gaps in the food chain that the cephalopods fill. A warming ocean can speed up cephalopod development, so population growth is more rapid, and cephalopods have such short lifespans that they are readily adaptable to change. A larger number also eats more food, and begins to outcompete any surviving fish.

Even so, scientists point out that cephalopods are not taking over the world, and that all manner of other factors could come into play to limit numbers. For one thing, shorter life cycles could mean individuals missing annual mating aggregations. For another, there is fishing for squid and octopus by humans, and most cephalopods have cannibalistic relatives. There is always competition in one form or another keeping things in check. As one marine biologist noted, 'I don't know whether we'll eat them first or they'll start eating each other.'

Policing Highways

Sharks, like their bony fish cousins, are victims of overfishing. Scientists estimate that up to 100 million are caught each year, mainly for their fins, the principal ingredient in shark-fin soup. Some have their fins sliced off when they are still alive, and their bodies are thrown back into the sea, where each shark dies a slow and probably painful death. But stopping the shark fin trade and conserving sharks alone is not necessarily the answer. Ignoring the other species in their ecosystem is foolhardy (see p.125), and protecting them en route to wherever they are going is vital; after all, several species of sharks are long-distance travellers. They are protected while in the territorial waters of enlightened countries, but out in the big blue anything goes.

Shark biologist Jonathan Green, who has studied whale sharks for the past 20 years, is far from optimistic about their future. 'If fishing in general and shark finning in particular continues at the level that it's at, then there's absolutely no way that in fifty to one hundred years' time any shark species will still survive on the planet.'

It is Jonathan's research in the Galápagos Islands that features in Chapter 5, but, he is first to admit that, despite all the hard work, we still know so little about whale sharks, especially how many there are.

'We have absolutely no idea of the world population. We know that they're being fished at possibly a massive rate. They may be taken by the thousands, and possibly the tens of thousands, a year. If that is true, we don't know how long they can stand that kind of fishing pressure.'

And protecting them is not going to be easy. 'Whale sharks are global voyagers. They perhaps go from one ocean to another. There's connectivity between populations in the Indian, Atlantic and Pacific oceans, but given the enormous size of the oceans, we can't simply say we'll protect the entire ocean surface. We have to choose specific areas – marine parks, marine protected areas, and, more importantly, marine corridors.'

Linking these conservation areas together with marine corridors is one way to help migrants like whale sharks, but first scientists need to locate the hotspots, and, after years of satellite tagging and tracking, Jonathan believes he has found one that is important to whale sharks.

'We have data that goes over a number of months, and during that time they are swimming several thousand miles across the ocean, and some are heading for a small speck in the Pacific Ocean – Darwin's Arch in the Galápagos Islands.

We've got in excess of a thousand individuals coming through the area of Darwin's Arch every season, and that could be a conservative figure. It's

HOMING BEACON (above) Darwin's Arch in the Galápagos Islands is a favoured destination for many species of sharks.

quite feasible that they travel halfway round the world to reach this tiny little rock in the Pacific Ocean. All of the evidence and all of the data that we're gathering is critical to protect areas such as Galápagos, but also the marine corridors between here and the other hotspots around the world to which they are travelling.'

Some Like It Hot … But Most Don't

Protecting hotspots and corridors will be to no avail, however, if we cannot come to terms with one chemical that, in modern times, has a profound effect on our lives and the lives of every living thing on the planet. It's carbon dioxide, and we have an uncomfortable relationship with it.

On the one hand, it is essential for all photosynthesising organisms, whether they are grass, giant redwoods or part of the phytoplankton, and, as these life forms are at the bottom of their respective food chains, almost every other living thing on Earth is dependent on it too. On the other hand, too much of it is not a good thing, and one of the biggest problems facing the world today is that we are producing too much of it.

About 36.4 billion tonnes of carbon dioxide is released into the atmosphere each year, a process faster than experienced on Earth for many millions of years, and mainly because of our reliance on fossil fuels – coal, oil, and natural gas. They are formed from the breakdown of organic

WATER, WATER ... (above) Icebergs and ice floes on which to haul out are at a premium in the waters off Svalbard, even in February, due partly to an influx of warm Atlantic waters, but, increasingly nowadays, to global warming.

ICE REFUGE (below) A mother polar bear and her cubs on a large iceberg off Baffin Island, Canada, in summer.

materials, such as the remains of ancient plants and animals. When they are burned in the internal combustion engines of automobiles and trucks or in factories and electricity power stations, they release carbon dioxide, which is a 'greenhouse gas'. Greenhouse gases trap heat in the atmosphere, like the glass in a greenhouse. The result is not hard to understand: the atmosphere heats up.

Data collected from eighty national weather services, according to the World Meteorological Organisation (WMO), reveals 2016 to have been the hottest year on record. In the same twelve months atmospheric carbon dioxide rose to a new high, warm moist air spilled into the Arctic, leading to a shift in atmospheric circulation patterns, the Arctic's winter sea ice recorded a new low, global sea levels rose to record levels, and global ocean heating was the highest on record. These 'extreme and unusual' trends have continued into 2017.

And this has not been a one-off series of events. WMO also reveals that the five hottest years on record have occurred since 2011, and indicates that the rising temperatures are strongly linked to human activities, especially the burning of fossil fuels. It has led the World Climate Research Programme Director at WMO to remark that 'we are now in truly uncharted territory.'

Ghost Reefs

When Alexander Vail was diving with his coral trout and octopus pals at Lizard Island, about 90 kilometres northeast of Cooktown, in the northern part of Australia's Great Barrier Reef, the elation following his successful research (see p.18) was tempered by the disturbing events that followed. On emerging from the water after a dive on the reef, Alexander noticed that the water was a few degrees warmer than usual, but it was at the beginning of spring and warm water was not expected so early in the year.

'What is happening here,' explains Alexander, 'is that the water has been much warmer than normal, and this means the algae that live inside the corals start to create toxic chemicals. The coral can't stand having the algae any more, so it has to expel them. These algae help provide food for the coral, through photosynthesis, and they are what gives the coral its colour. So, when coral bleaches, it goes completely white. The coral can survive for a few weeks, even when it's white. It's not dead, but if the warm temperatures stay for too long, the coral starves to death.'

And this was no ordinary event. It was linked to El Niño, the warm phase of a climate cycle in the Pacific Ocean that has an impact on weather systems all over the world. In some parts, combined with a warming climate, it drove up air and sea temperatures during 2015 and 2016 to record levels.'

The bleaching has been the worst in the history of the Great Barrier Reef. About 90 per cent of the branching coral out here on Lizard Island are dead. It's absolutely terrible. It's a huge blow to the reef. The coral reef provides protection for thousands of different species, and the grouper and octopus will die without the fish that live amongst the corals.

'It's incredibly bad to see the area you have dived on since you were a little kid just turn to rubble. That is horrible. I cried in my facemask when I saw the devastation from bleaching. It's been pretty bad.'

Following this disastrous event, a survey of the Great Barrier Reef in early 2017 revealed that the reef has suffered significant bleaching again, the second successive year for widespread bleaching caused by elevated water temperatures, and the first time a large part of the reef has been hit twice in less than twelve months. And the same is occurring on many other reefs in the tropics, with a projection by an international team of oceanographers – co-ordinated by the University of Miami and published in the journal *Scientific Reports* – that 99 per cent of the world's tropical coral reefs will undergo serious bleaching during the twenty-first century.

BLEACHING (above) Corals bleaching at Lizard Island, Great Barrier Reef.

So the outlook is distinctly gloomy for coral reefs, especially the Great Barrier Reef. For them, climate change is not a future threat. It's happening here and now, and rising water temperature is only part of the story.

Acid Seas

Carbon dioxide is changing the chemistry of the oceans. About a third of all the carbon dioxide emitted into the atmosphere is absorbed directly into the sea, where it reacts with the water to form a weak acid. Before the industrialised age, chemicals dissolved in river water, which was washed into the sea, neutralising the acid, but now we are generating so much carbon dioxide and so rapidly that the rivers cannot keep up. It means that as the carbon dioxide in our atmosphere increases, so does the acidity of the oceans, first in the surface waters and then, with mixing, down into the deep sea.

The figures involved seem small. The pH of the oceans before the Industrial Revolution was 8.2 (pH 7 is neutral), making it slightly basic. Now it is about 8.1 and falling, but this drop actually represents a 25 per cent increase in acidity that has occurred in a couple of hundred years. Projections to the end of the century indicate that the pH could drop a further 0.5. Similar natural shifts might take tens of thousands of years, during which marine life has had time to adapt. At the University of Miami, Professor Chris Langdon has been studying this worrying trend.

'The shells of molluscs are made of calcium carbonate, and the acid dissolves them, and, as they dissolve, they shrink and start to disappear. This applies to corals too. The entire framework of the reef is built of calcium carbonate, the same material the shells are made of. As that dissolves the homes for everything that lives in or on the reef are going to start to disappear too.'

This is something that Professor Langdon and his colleagues expected to see in the distant future – not now.

'The northern parts of the Florida reef tract are starting to dissolve, which is a big surprise, because we didn't think this would happen until the end of this century.'

To see what might happen in the distant future, University of Chicago researchers have been studying mussel shells on the coast of Washington state. The waters here are unusual. Winds blowing parallel to the coast have strengthened due to global warming, so upwellings are bringing up more deep water and nutrients to the surface. The deep water here is in a bit of a cul-de-sac, where carbon dioxide has built up and ventilation of the bottom layers is poor, so it is naturally more acidic than elsewhere in the ocean. It means coastal waters are more acidic too, and research has shown that the drop in pH has a significant impact on mussel shells, and it's measurable.

Shells collected by Native Americans about a thousand years ago, which have been lodged in museums, are about 28 per cent thicker than modern shells. Although this is not a product of present-day acidification due to raised carbon dioxide levels in the atmosphere, it does give an idea what could happen elsewhere in the future.

'Ocean acidification is disastrous for any animal with a shell,' Professor Langdon points out, 'and, as shellfish start to die out, it'll have a huge impact on all the animals that rely on them for food – fish, seals and us.'

Life in general is sensitive to even quite small changes in pH. Human blood, for example, has a normal pH of 7.35–7.45, and a drop of as little as 0.2–0.3 can put someone into a coma, and they can even die. In the ocean, it means that some forms of marine life will be unable to respire, reproduce, or grow. The last time this happened on a big scale was about 55 million years ago, when many animals in the ocean died out. Long before that, about 250 million years ago, intense volcanism caused, amongst other things, some serious ocean acidification, when 90 per cent of marine species became extinct – the so-called 'time of great dying'. Today, events in prehistory could be repeating themselves, and there is no doubt who the culprit is this time.

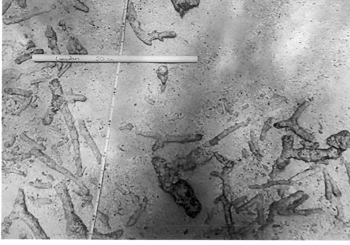

'There is absolute categorical proof that the carbon dioxide that's causing this is manmade,' says Professor Langdon. 'The isotopic composition of fossil fuels is a unique chemical fingerprint, which is completely different from other sources of carbon dioxide that are being added to the atmosphere, so we can see in the water and in the atmosphere that the carbon dioxide cannot be coming from natural causes: its coming from fossil fuels.'

It's a bleak picture, but there's hope.

ACID ATTACK (above) Pictures from the University of Miami show how increasingly acidic seawater is dissolving the limestone framework of Carysfort Reef in the Florida Keys.

'This future does not have to play out. It's up to us. All we have to do is reduce our carbon dioxide emissions. We can switch to renewable fuel – wind and solar instead of fossil fuels. The catastrophe could be avoided.'

And acidification is not the only catastrophe caused by elevated carbon dioxide levels that humankind is staring in the face.

Crisis at the Water's Edge

Around 40 per cent of the world's human population lives within 100 kilometres of the coast, and more are moving there. The Centre for Climate Systems Research at Columbia University has calculated that, from now until 2025, 35 per cent of people living at a safe distance from the coast will move into the danger zone, placing an increasing burden on coastlines, and exposing the homes and businesses of 2.75 billion people to the risk of flooding and storm damage if sea levels rise significantly – and the scary thing is, they are! Sea levels are rising faster than at any time during the past 3,000 years. One of the hotspots is the western Pacific, close to Guam and its leaping blennies. Here the sea level has risen 15 centimetres in just 20 years, a rate that is likely to come to other parts of the world in coming decades.

A study by the National Oceanographic Centre in Liverpool suggests that an increase in global temperature of 2°C above the pre-industrial temperature (and we already reached 1.1°C during 2016) could be reached in 2040–2050 with an average sea level rise of 20 centimetres. This is on top of the 20-centimetre rise that has occurred already since 1880. However, 90 per cent of coastal areas will experience higher sea levels than

CREEPING CONCRETE (above)
The Chinese city of Shenzen dominates the foreshore on the right, while commercial fish and shrimp ponds are located on the left. Both are close to the internationally important Mai Po marshes of Hong Kong.

average, such as the Atlantic coast of North America with a 40-centimetre rise. This unevenness is due to ocean dynamics and changes of gravity associated with the redistribution of water. Above this 2°C threshold, however, things start to go awry in a big way.

If the warming continues, and the global temperature increases to 5°C then, by 2100, the average sea level rise could be a metre or maybe two, but again it will not be the same all over the world. Some areas – including the sites of many cities, such as New York and Miami, and small island states – could see a rise of between 1 and 1.8 metres, and the models are constantly being revised upwards.

A knock-on effect of this is how we treat our coasts. Coasts are being squeezed. On the one side are rising sea levels, while on the other more sea defences are being built to protect low-lying areas. The result is that the coast is being hardened and raised, so coasts are changing faster than any other part of the ocean, with the greatest loss of wildlife habitats.

Coastal habitats are heavily undervalued. As often as not, they are seen merely as places ripe for reclamation and development, rather than for nature. During the past 20 years, for example, China has lost 70 per cent of its coastal habitats, such as mudflats, reclaiming the land for building developments and aquaculture. The disappearance of such ecologically important places has meant fewer nursery sites for marine life, poorer water quality, and a loss of feeding sites for migratory birds. And on coasts where defences or developments are not an issue, the intertidal zone is faced with a new dynamic. As sea levels rise, the intertidal zone will move inland. It will give 'high tide' a whole new meaning.

If all that's not enough, there's the news that these things cannot be switched off like an electric light. Even if we stopped manmade carbon dioxide emissions tomorrow, the effects do not go away immediately, according to a study by the Massachusetts Institute of Technology and Canada's Simon Fraser University; indeed, they will continue to build for a while before reversing. The research revealed that greenhouse gases, such as carbon dioxide, contribute to sea level rise through thermal expansion over much longer timescales than their atmospheric lifetime. It means that even if we could curb the burning of fossil fuels, the impact of human-produced carbon dioxide emissions on sea level rise could persist for centuries. Some models predict that we are already committed to a 3-metre rise over the next few hundred years.

Good News... At Last

Frustrating though it may be that many parts of our oceans have been rapidly deteriorating, it doesn't have to be this way. All it takes are a few strong-willed people to help bring about change, and sometimes it is the small things that have the greatest impact.

During the late nineteenth and early twentieth centuries, Monterey Bay on the Pacific coast of the USA was a disaster area. Hunters had exterminated most of the sea otters and visiting gray whales. With the sea otters gone, abalone thrived, but a burgeoning shellfish industry suddenly disappeared due to overfishing less than 15 years after it had begun. Next it was the turn of sardines, but the sardine canneries dumped so much waste into the Bay that it became an industrial cesspit. By the time John Steinbeck published *Cannery Row* in 1945, the sardine fishery was also collapsing, due to overfishing and a change in the ocean currents. The Bay was in terminal decline, yet today it is a pristine marine environment with kelp forests, fish, seabirds, sea otters, harbour seals, dolphins, elephant seal breeding beaches, killer whales, and migrating gray and humpback whales. Its transformation was down partly to a very determined young lady who had moved to the area in 1899.

Julia Platt gained a PhD in marine zoology at Germany's University of Freiburg because, at the time, American universities did not admit women to study for such a degree. Even then, she could not pursue her chosen career in the USA, so eventually she took up local politics. In their book *The Death and Life of Monterey Bay*, Stephen Palumbi and Carolyn Sotka reveal how Platt became so frustrated with the way the Bay had been treated that, at the age of 74, she ran for mayor at Pacific Grove and won. She persuaded the State governor to pass a law that enabled Pacific Grove to manage its own waterfront and adjacent parts of Monterey Bay. It was the first, and, indeed, the last Californian city to gain the right, and, with this legal backing Platt was able to create two marine refuges. Almost singlehandedly she had started to put this stretch of coast back on the road to recovery, changing people's attitudes to the Bay and the way it is used. With a collapse of the sardine industry, the closure of the canneries, and, crucially, the return in 1962 of the sea otter, a keystone species (see p.153), the Bay was reseeded with the marine life that had been protected in Julia Platt's marine refuges. Platt herself did not live to see the fruits of her labours: she died in 1935, long before the real recovery took place.

The Bay, however, received another boost when, in 1984, David Packard, co-founder of Hewlett-Packard, provided the initial financial

PINNIPED PALS (opposite) A pair of California sea lions resting on the shores of Monterey Bay.

backing for the Monterey Bay Aquarium, built in honour of Edward Ricketts – 'Doc' in Steinbeck's *Cannery Row*. Monterey Bay had become a place for research, conservation, and contemplation, rather than overfishing, destruction, and neglect.

Steinbeck also wrote, in *The Log from the Sea of Cortez*, about the ancient coral reefs at Cabo Pulmo, at the southern tip of the Baja California Peninsula. They were teeming with life in the 1950s, but by the early 1990s, like Monterey Bay, they were overfished and barren. This time, the Castro family championed the sea. Three generations of fishermen made the momentous decision to stop fishing the reef, and they persuaded the local fishing community to follow suit. Then they lobbied the government to protect the reef.

In 1995, the Cabo Pulmo National Park was created and the fishermen ensured the entire area of the park became a no-fishing zone. By 2009,

REFUELLING STOP (above) Gray whales once more visit the Bay, snacking on mysid shrimps amongst the giant kelp, before continuing on their long journey from Baja California to the Arctic.

GOLDEN RAYS (above) A school of Pacific or golden cownose rays are on migration through the Cabo Pulmo National Park. The rays have a 'wingspan' of about 70 centimetres. They travel in large schools, following the drop-off at the edge of the reef.

many species of fish had returned, including sharks, manta rays and the endangered gulf grouper. It hadn't happened overnight, but, after 14 years of protection, the biomass of the reef had increased by a staggering 463 per cent, with fish stocks five times larger than in the fished areas nearby. It was the largest increase observed anywhere in the world, and all down to the will of the local community. Local folk gained by an increase in the number of tourists visiting the area, and, by a ripple effect, neighbouring fishing areas, outside the reef, came to have more fish to catch too. It was a win-win situation.

What these two stories tell us is that, when given half a chance, the ocean is resilient. It can bounce back. Reduce the fishing pressure, create unpolluted no-take areas and our seas will begin to restore themselves. Protect and better manage the global ecosystem and the ocean will recover.

We have come a long way on this ocean journey. We have crossed the open ocean, explored coasts and coral reefs, weaved in and out of the underwater forests and meadows, and dived down to the bottom of the deep sea, but, as befitting, we leave the last word on this underwater realm to Sir David Attenborough, who has seen at first hand the marvels of the ocean, been humbled by its majesty, excited by its diversity and challenged by the ingenuity of the creatures that live there ... but he is deeply disturbed about its future.

'In my lifetime, there have been great changes in the ocean. Species of fish that we once took for granted have disappeared, and whole ecosystems are on the verge of destruction. We are at a unique stage in our history. Never before have we had such an awareness of what we are doing to the planet, and never before have we had the power to do something about it. Surely we have a responsibility to care for our blue planet. The future of humanity, and, indeed, of all of life on Earth, now depends on us.'

FRAGILE WALL (opposite) Sunset over a coral reef on Réunion in the Indian Ocean. The reef protects the western coast from storms, and the challenge for the recently established Marine National Park is to balance its health with the needs of a burgeoning tourist industry.

Index

Acknowledgements

Firstly, we'd like to thank Michael Bright for his considerable help and dedication in shaping this book.

The stories featured in these pages could not be told without the huge efforts of countless scientists, marine biologists, oceanographers, undersea explorers and marine researchers. We are deeply indebted to the entire scientific community, as without new science we would not have new stories to tell.

We would like to thank those scientists who have collaborated with us in the discovery of new behaviours and we wish them well in the publication of their papers. Special thanks go to our series advisors, Dr Callum Roberts, Professor Alex Rogers and Dr Steve Simpson.

Thank you also to the Universities, Oceanographic Institutions and Marine Labs that hosted us at the start of production. In particular, in the USA: Marine Biological Laboratory, Woods Hole Oceanographic Institution, Scripps Institution of Oceanography, and Schmidt Ocean Institute; and in the UK: the National Oceanography Centre.

All work at sea carries inherent risks. We are grateful to everyone – the dive masters, dive supervisors, safety divers and boat captains and crews – who has kept our teams safe.

The exploration of the deep ocean is logistically complex and hugely challenging. We are very grateful to the Dalio Ocean Initiative and Alucia Productions, as well as the crew of MV Alucia and her submarines Nadir and Deep Rover, for their help and support in gaining access to the deep seas of the Pacific, Atlantic and Southern oceans, and to the Rebikoff-Niggeler Foundation for their help in the deep sea off the Azores.

We are hugely grateful to the cinematographers, camera operators, drone operators, stills photographers, technicians and edit assistants who have captured and managed such stunning imagery.

And lastly, we'd like to thank our production team – the makers of Blue Planet II – for five years of intense and challenging work, allowing us to create a portrait of the oceans like never before.

Mark Brownlow & James Honeyborne

13 5 7 9 10 8 6 4 2

BBC Books, an imprint of Ebury Publishing
20 Vauxhall Bridge Road,
London SW1V 2SA

BBC Books is part of the Penguin Random House group of companies whose addresses can be found at global.penguinrandomhouse.com

Penguin Random House UK

Copyright ã Mark Brownlow and James Honeyborne 2017

Mark Brownlow and James Honeyborne have asserted their right to be identified as the authors of this Work in accordance with the Copyright, Designs and Patents Act 1988

This book is published to accompany the television series entitled Blue Planet II first broadcast on BBC One in 2017.

Executive producer: James Honeyborne
Series producer: Mark Brownlow

First published by BBC Books in 2017
www.penguin.co.uk

A CIP catalogue record for this book is available from the British Library

9781849909679

Commissioning Editor: Albert DePetrillo
Project Editor: Bethany Wright
Picture Research: Laura Barwick
Image Grading: Stephen Johnson, www.copyrightimage.co.uk
Design: Bobby Birchall, Bobby&Co
Production: Antony Heller

Printed and bound in Italy by Printer Trento

Penguin Random House is committed to a sustainable future for our business, our readers and our planet. This book is made from Forest Stewardship Council® certified paper.

MIX
Paper from responsible sources
FSC® C018179

SCIENTIFIC ADVISORS
Adrian Flynn
Alan Jamieson
Alex Rogers
Alex Schnell
Alison Kock
Andrew Thurber
Angela Ward
Angela Ziltener
Asha de Vos
Audun Rikardsen
Benoit Pirenne
Bernd Wursig
Bob 'Coop' Cooper
Brendan Godley
Bruce Robison
Callum Roberts
Carlie Wiener
Cathy Lucas
Ceri Lewis
Chandra Salgado Kent
Charles Fisher
Charlie Maule
Cherisse Du Preez
Chris Langdon
Craig Foster
Craig Smith
Cynthia Klepadlo
Daniel Fornari
Daphne Cuvelier
David Cade
David Green
David Johns
David Lusseau
Deborah Kelley
Deborah Thiele
Don R. Levitan
Douglas Syme
Edith Widder

Emily Duncan
Erik Ivins
Etienne Rastoin
Eve Jourdain
Fabio De Leo
Franklin Ariaga
Guy Stevens
Huw Griffiths
Ivan Rodriguez
Jake Levenson
Jakob Scwendner
James Gardner
James Kerry
Jamie Craggs
Jamie Walker
Jason Fowler
Jeffrey Drazen
Jim Darling
Jochen Zaeschmar
John McCosker
Jon Copley
Jonathan Green
Jorge Fontes
Jose Lachat
Josh Stewart
Julian Finn
Kate Moran
Katrin Linse
Kerry Howell
Kim Fulton-Bennett
Kim Juniper
Kit Kovacs
Kyra Schlining
Larry Crowder
Lars Kleivane
Laurenz Thomsen
Leif Nottestad
Leopoldo Moro
Leslie Elliott

Leslie Hart
Lloyd Peck
Louise Allcock
Lucy Quinn
Luke Rendell
Malcolm McCulloch
Maria Baker
Maria Dias
Mark Belchier
Mark Eakin
Mark Erdmann
Mark Norman
Meghan Jones
Michael H Graham
Michael Rasheed
Mike Meredith
Ove Hoegh-Guldberg
Paul Sikkel
Pelayo Salinas de Leon
Phil Trathan
Randall Wells
Rich Palmer
Richard Phillips
Robert Carney
Rogelio Herra
Roger Hanlon
Roldan Munoz
Roldan Valverde
Roy L. Caldwell
Sam Burrell
Samantha Joye
Sarah Mckay-Strobel
Sergio Pucci
Shane Gero
Simon Pierce
Stephanie Bush
Steve Haddock
Steve Katz
Steve Simpson

Stuart Banks
Terry Ord
Thomas Jefferson
Tim Tinker
Timothy Shank
Tiu Similia
Tom Kwasnitschka
Tone Kristin Reiertsen
Tracey Sutton
Verena Tunnicliffe
Victor Zykov
Vidal Martin
Volker Ratmeyer
William Chadwick
William Gilly
Yannis Papastamatiou
Yvonne Sadovy

CAMERA TEAM
Alex Vail
Alfredo Barroso
Andrea Casini
Andy Brandy Casagrande IV
Barrie Britton
Blair Monk
Charlie Stoddart
Chris Bryans
Chris Sammut
Cinemacopter
Craig Foster
Dan Paris
Daniel Zatz
David Reichert
Didier Noirot
Espen Rekdal
Gail Jenkinson
Gavin Thurston

Helipov
Hugh Miller
Ivan Agerton
Jack Johnston
Janssen Powers
Jason Sturgis
João Paulo Krajewski
Joe Platko
John Aitchison
John Shier
Johnny Rogers
Jonathan Clay
Kevin Flay
Kieran Donnelly
Mark Macewan
Mark Payne-Gill
Mark Sharman
Mark Van Coller
Mateo Willis
Matt Norman
Morne Hardenberg
Nick Guy
Nuno Sa
Pascal Lorent
Patrick Dykstra
Paul Williams
Peter Nearhos
Rafa Hererro
Rene Heuzey
Richard Karoliussen
Richard Kirby
Richard Robinson
Richard Stevenson
Richard Wollocombe
Rick Rosenthal
Rob Franklin
Rob Whitworth
Rod Clarke
Roger Horrocks
Roger Munns
Shayne Thomson
Steve Hathaway
Ted Giffords
Tim Shepherd
Toby Strong
Tom Fitz
Trent Ellis
Yasushi Okumura

WITH SPECIAL THANKS
Adrian Skerrett
Advanced Imaging
    and Visualization
    Laboratory
Akihito Yamada
Alex Tattersall
Alexia Graba Landry
American Museum of
    Natural History
Andrew Downey
Annie Murray
Arctic Rays
Ari Friedlaender
Athena Dinar
Audun Rikardsen
Aurelie Duhec
Australian Institute of
    Marine Science
Australian Museum's
    Lizard Island
    Research Station
Bamfield Marine
    Sciences Centre
Benj Youngson
Bill and Annie Weeks
Bob Cranston

Bob Lamerson
Bob Talbot
Bonnie Waycott
Brett Illingworth
British Antarctic Survey
Bryan Kilback
Buddhika Dhayarathne
California Academy of
    Sciences
Callum Brown
Casey Dunn Laboratory
Ceri MacLure
Chad Tamis
Chase Weir
Chris Jones
Civil Aviation Authority
    of Sri Lanka
Customised Animal
    Tracking Solutions
Dan Laffoley
Daniel Copeland
Dave Blackham
David Booth
David Graham
David Sullivan
Dean Martin
Deirdre O'Driscoll
Discover Dominica
    Authority
DOER
Dolphin Watch Alliance
Dominica Film Office
Doug Allan
Ecosystem Impacts of
    Oil and Gas Inputs to
    the Gulf
Ed McNichol
Einar Eliassen
Elizabeth White
Environs Kimberley
Errol and Marcella
    Harris
Etienne Rastoin
Exposure Labs
Fabrice Jaine
Fernando Luchsinger
Frank Wirth
Franklin Arreaga
Kirsten and Joachim
    Jakobsen
Fundacion Charles
    Darwin
Galapagos National
    Parks
Garrett Mcnamara
Geoff Lloyd
Gerald Nicholas
Gerhard Lauscher
Godfrey Merlen
Gordon Leicester
Government of South
    Georgia & the South
    Sandwich Islands
Grace Frank
Grande Riviere Anglican
    Primary School
Great Barrier Reef
    Marine Park Authority
Gregory Bogdan
Howard Hall
Huu-Ay-Aht First
    Nations
Iwan Muhani
Jaap Barendrecht
James Cameron
James Leyland
Japan Underwater Films

Jason Isley
Jason Ribbink
Jason Roberts
    Productions
Jemal Guerrero
Jennifer Hile
Jennifer Lee
Jim Standing, Fourth
    Element
John and *Jenny*
    Edmondson
John Ellerbrock,
    Gates
John Pennekamp State
    Park
John Rumney
Jonathan Watts
Jorge Leal
José Masaquisa
Josiane Dalcourt
Julian Gutt
Julian Pepperall
Jung-Goo Myoung
Justin Marshall
Kelvin Murray
Kim Juniper
Koji Nakamura
Lawson Barnes
Leah Sokolowsky
Leif Nøttestad
Leigh Marsh
Len Peters
Leon Deschamps
Leslie Elliott
Liisa Juuti
Lily Kozmian-Ledward
Lisa Kelly
Louisiana State
    University
Luke English
Lyle Berzins
M/V Alucia Submersible
    Team
M/V Umbra Captain and
    Crew
Marine Biological
    Association
Marine Institute
Marissa Fox, Executive
    Director of Oceans
    Forward
Mark Belchier
Mark Dalio
Marten Bril
Martin How
Mary Summerill
Masahiko Sakata
Mauricio Handler
Maya Santangelo
Michael Stadermann
Michelle Hart
Mike DeRoos
Mike Kasic
Mike McDowell
Mike Meredith
Ministry of Agriculture
    and Fisheries, Fisheries
    Division Dominica
Ministry of Agriculture
    and Forestry, Wildlife
    & Parks Division,
    Dominica
Ministry of Defense of
    Sri Lanka
Mohan Sandhu
Monterey Bay Aquarium
    Research Institute

Nancy Black
National Oceanic
    and Atmospheric
    Administration
National Oceanography
    Centre
Natural History Museum
Nature Trails
Neil Brock
Newcastle University
Nicholas Pedrocci
Nick Pitt, Farm Studio
Nico Ghersinich
Nicolas Pilcher
Nils Arne Saebo
Niv Froman, Manta
    Trust
Norwegian Orca Survey
Nova Southeastern
    University
NRK
Ocean Exploration Trust
Ocean Networks Canada
Ocean Research
    and Conservation
    Association
Olli Barbé
Oregon State University
Pang Quong
Paul Collins
Paul Seagrove
Paul Yancey
Peggy Stap
Pelayo Salinas de Leon
Pennsylvania State
    University
Per Borre
Pete Bassett
Peter King
Peter Kraft
Phil Sammet
Plymouth University
PT Hirschfield
R/V Falkor Captain and
    Crew
Ray Dalio
Redboats
Richard Bull
Richard Herrmann
Richard Phillips
Robert Pitman
Roberto Pepolas
ROPOS
Rowan Aitchison
Sally Snow
Samantha Andrzejaczek
San Francisco
    University Quito
Sarah Dwyer
Schmidt Ocean
    Institute
School of Chemistry,
    University of Bristol
Scott Carnahan
SeaMaster Costa Rica
    team
Sheila Patek
Sheree Marris
Simon George
Simon Villamar
Sina Kreicker
Sri Lanka Coast Guard
Sri Lanka Department
    of Wildlife
    Conservation
Sri Lanka National Film
    Corporation

Sri Lanka Navy
St Luke's Primary
    School, Pointe
    Michel, Dominica
Stanford University
Stefan Andrews
Steve Benjamin
Sub C Imaging
Suzanne Lockhart
The Ocean Agency
Thomas Furey
Tim North
Tiu Simila
Tomas Lundalf
Tony Bramley, fixer
Tony Wu
Tore Tien
Torre Lein
University of Galway
University of Georgia
University Of Hawai'i At
    Manoa
University of Miami
    Rosenstiel School
    of Marine and
    Atmospheric Science
University of Oxford
University Of The
    Azores
University of Victoria
University of Western
    Australia
Vincent Pieribone
Wayne Mcfee
Woods Hole
    Oceanographic
    Institute
Y.Zin Kim
Yvette Oosthuizen
Zara-Louise Cowan

PRODUCTION TEAM

Sir David Attenborough

Tom McDonald

Alexandra Fennell
Chiara Minchin
Dan Beecham
Daniel Prosser
Ester de Roij
Francesca Maxwell
Jack Delf
James Taggart
Jamie Love
Jenny Foulkes
Joanna Stead
Joanna Verity
Jodie Allt
Joe Hope
Joe Stevens
Joe Treddenick
John Chambers
John Ruthven
Jonathan Smith
Joseph Fenton
Karmen Summers
Katie Hall
Katrina Steele
Marcus Coyle
Matthew Brierley
Melanie Thomas
Miles Barton
Natalie Cross
Nicole Kruysse

Orla Doherty
Rachel Butler
Saijal Patel
Sandra Forbes
Sarah Conner
Simon Cross
Sophie Morgan
Sylvia Mukasa
Will Ridgeon
Yoland Bosiger
Zeenat Shah

POST PRODUCTION
Films at 59
Miles Hall

MUSIC
Bleeding Fingers
Catherine Grimes
Hans Zimmer
Jacob Shea
Jasha Klebe
Natasha Klebe
Natasha Pullin
Russell Emanuel

FILM EDITORS
Dave Pearce
Matt Meech
Nigel Buck
Pete Brownlee
Andrew Mort
Jack Johnston
Robin Lewis

ONLINE EDITORS
Frank Ketterer
Wes Hibberd

DUBBING EDITORS
Kate Hopkins
Tim Owens

DUBBING MIXER
Graham Wild

COLOURIST
Adam Inglis

GRAPHIC DESIGN
BDH Creative

BBC WORLDWIDE
Patricia Fearnley
Monica Hayes
Hayley Moore
Rebecca Hyde